At the Crossroads

At the Crossroads

The Remarkable CPA Firm That Nearly Crashed, Then Soared

Gale Crosley, C.P.A.

and

Debbie Stover

WILEY

John Wiley & Sons, Inc.

Some material in this book previously appeared, in altered form, in *Accounting Today; CPA Practice Management Forum*, a monthly journal published by CCH, a Wolters Kluwer business; and *Partner Advantage Advisory*, published by Martha Sawyer and August Aquila.

For more information about Wiley products, visit our Web site at http://www.wiley.com.

Library of Congress Cataloging-in-Publication Data:

Crosley, Gale.

 At the crossroads: the remarkable CPA firm that nearly crashed, then soared/Gale Crosley and Debbie Stover.

  p. cm.

 The story of a mythical Minneapolis CPA firm, Crandall & Potter, a composite based on various firms the author has worked with as a consultant.

ISBN 978-0-470-14817-4 (cloth)

1. Accounting firms—Management. 2. Organizational change. 3. Organizational effectiveness. I. Stover, Debbie. II. Title. III. Title: CPA firm that nearly crashed, then soared.

HF5628.C73 2008

657.068 – dc22   2007036514

10 9 8 7 6 5 4 3 2 1

To God our Father
Who has given special gifts to each one of us,
so that we can help each other to do His good work on earth.
And who has given me such rich blessings in my family:
Erica, Jeff, Kim, Kristin, and husband Steve
G.C.

for Chris and,
always, throughout time,
for Cleveland
D.S.

ABOUT THE AUTHORS

GALE GUNDERSON CROSLEY, CPA, was selected one of the Most Recommended Consultants in *Inside Public Accounting*'s "Best of the Best" annual survey for the fourth consecutive year, was named one of the Top 100 Most Influential People in Accounting by *Accounting Today* for the last two years. She is founder and principal of Crosley + Company, an Atlanta-based firm dedicated to helping CPA firms achieve "the business discipline of practice growth." Gale has a degree in accounting from the University of Akron (Ohio) and is a CPA in Ohio and Georgia. Her background includes nearly 30 years of business development and senior management in the corporate world, including IBM and several small technology companies. She has been responsible for developing high-performance rainmaking organizations, bringing more than 30 services and products to market, and closing dozens of multimillion-dollar and smaller opportunities. Gale can be reached at *gcrosley@crosleycompany.com*, by phone at 770-399-9995, or on her Web site, *crosleycompany .com*. Gale lives in Atlanta with her husband, Steve, and their children.

DEBBIE STOVER is a freelance writer with extensive writing and publishing credentials. She served as chief editor of two business newsletters published by McGraw-Hill, as senior editor of four magazines published by Advanstar Inc., and has written innumerable non-bylined pieces that have appeared in publications including the *Washington Post* and the *New York Times*. For several years, she served as legislative and press aide to United States Congressman Ron Paul. She lives and runs in St. Louis, aided by her partner, Chris, and their mostly furry family. Debbie can be reached at *ds@DebbieStover.com.*

CONTENTS

INTRODUCTION

The last few years of my career have been the most interesting and fulfilling I've ever experienced. Since I started working again with CPAs and their firms, I feel like I've "come home." These are my people.

When I began my career as an auditor, working for Arthur Andersen and then Price Waterhouse, I was constantly being reprimanded for talking too much to the clients. Eventually I found my way into corporate America, working in the "growth" disciplines: sales, marketing, and product management. After 25 years, circumstances caused me to return to my roots—but this time my clients are CPA firms. And this time, talking is allowed!

In returning to the profession, I made a very interesting discovery. I found that the few largest CPA firms had developed sophisticated approaches to driving and managing growth. But I also found that outside this handful of largest firms, there was little understanding of how to sustain efficient and effective growth. Most CPA firms just "got out there and did good work." There's nothing wrong with that, of course, but it is *not* the whole story, because it doesn't take into account the processes, methodologies, and consistent execution of best practices that are so necessary to smart growth.

Not only leading CPA firms, but corporate America as a whole, is way ahead of most CPAs in understanding and managing effective growth approaches. And with the paucity of CPAs, we can scarcely afford to waste time on approaches that don't work!

We have only to look outside our profession to identify the best techniques; there's no reason for trial and error or starting from scratch. But most CPAs haven't worked in corporate America, so they don't know this wealth of knowledge exists.

As I've consulted with CPA firms, helping them understand and implement these proven growth techniques, I've found the same issues cropping up, and seen recurring themes in terms of behaviors and levels of understanding. These themes, the people involved, and the success I've seen them ultimately achieve—using corporate America's growth techniques, adapted for the CPA environment—form the foundation of this book.

It's been great fun to breathe life into these characters. They're an amalgamation of people with whom I've worked in countless firms, where I've seen managing partners and partner groups grab the reins and craft their own wonderful destinies. The most fulfilling part of being a consultant lies in witnessing this transformation. In firms that make the commitment to grow, the firm grows as the people grow, and they reach their full potential together.

Finally, this book is about hope. Whether your firm is experiencing real growth or not—whether, to jump a few pages ahead, your story more closely resembles Alex's or Joe's—you will surely recognize the partners and others you meet here. You may wince once or twice, but I think you'll also smile along the way. I know you'll go away understanding that, armed with the right knowledge, you can steer your own firm into a bright and prosperous future.

—*Gale Crosley*

CAST OF CHARACTERS

At Our Mythical Firm:

The Main Partners:

Joe Abriola, managing partner of Crandall & Potter, a Minneapolis CPA firm that's going nowhere

Eric King, the firm's brightest niche rainmaker; he's still young, so no one takes him too seriously

Charles Krueger, the auditor's auditor

Kevin McCoy, the tax guru

Harold Brumlow, who's retired in place, the firm fossil

. . .and assorted other partners, 24 in all, among them:

Ben Spencer, an outgoing guy with a sense of humor, but very nuts and bolts

Smith Smoot, smart, but a bit defensive about his name

Durwood Poole, a senior partner, he's solid but unexceptional

Frank Pierce, the original no-nonsense guy, who never has a good word to say

Matthew Hanover, the youngest partner, who's very earnest

Jake Billings, a young CPA who's never at a loss for words

Joshua Huberman, the quietest member of the firm

The Key Staff:

Jackie Brown, COO, efficient and by the book, she came up through the ranks

Tiff Hollister, marketing director, who does great brochures, but that's about it

Ty Dukes, third in a line of business developers, who's got no get up and go, but he's a terrific gladhander. What does he do all day?

Other Staff:

Sarah Brandeis, a senior tax manager

Josie Fitzmorris, a young manager in real estate

Thaddeus Cox, the mailroom supervisor

Earlier:

Albert Potter, founding partner (deceased)

Later:

Philip Van Landingham, new partner and audit segment leader

Michael Cunningham, business developer; Ty's very able successor

Lisa Olson, C&P's first-ever recruiting director

Elsewhere:

Alex Weinstein, of blockbusting Philadelphia CPA firm Weinstein & Federman

Katherine Witt, the very savvy director of practice growth at Alex's firm

PART I

NO DISCIPLINE, NO GROWTH

Some Bad News

Joe Abriola looked up from his desk as his favorite "son" in the firm, Eric King, slipped quietly into the room and took a seat.

Joe leaned back, linking his hands behind his head. "What's going on, Eric?"

Eric leaned forward, brought his hands up, and opened his mouth, but no sound came out at first. Finally he shook his head and spoke. "I feel bad about telling you this, Joe. I want you to know that up front."

"What's the problem?" Joe asked. "Is it a client?"

"No," Eric said, and then the words came skittering out of his mouth in a terrible rush. "It's the partners. It's a problem with the *partners*. *You've* got a great big problem with your partners." Eric paused. "And I don't think you even know it."

The Problem

Joe had leaned forward in his chair as Eric spoke, but now he settled back cautiously. "No," he said at length, "I'm not aware of any problem with the partners. What kind of problem?"

Eric took a moment to collect his thoughts, shook his head briefly, then spoke. "Joe, I want you to know, as I said, that I feel really uncomfortable doing this. You brought me into this firm, you've given me a terrific chance to succeed here, and . . . It feels, I don't know, not like disloyalty, but like . . . carrying tales, maybe. But I really think you need to know what's going on, and nobody else is going to tell you. So I feel like I'm elected."

"Spit it out, son," Joe said.

"It's like this," Eric said, leaning forward again, elbows on his knees. "There are these . . . I'd call them rumblings—and they're just sweeping through the partner group. I think they started with Harold and Kevin, but it seems like every day, one more person chimes in. We've got—what?—24 partners in this firm, and I swear half of them are grumbling about 'changes.' " Eric drew quotation marks around the word with his voice. "They say 'changes' need to be made. And at first it was generic, but now people are specifically mentioning you."

"All right," Joe said cautiously. "What kind of changes?"

Eric shifted in his chair uncomfortably. "To be perfectly honest, Joe, I'm afraid some of this may have started with me." Joe frowned, but Eric plunged ahead with his story.

"You remember last month, when I went to that niche meeting"— Eric had his own niche, health care, well in hand within the firm—"and they were talking about growth and comparing notes. And one guy's reporting eighteen-percent growth year to date at his firm, and the other fellow has twenty-one. One guy said his health care practice grew twenty-five percent last year!

"You remember I told you about that, right, Joe?" Eric pressed.

Joe nodded.

"Well, I mentioned it to some other people around here as well. And it turns out that I'm not the only person who's hearing it. We all know what started it—Sarbanes-Oxley back in '02—but it's gotten bigger since then, much bigger. It seems like every CPA firm in the country—or in Minneapolis, anyway—is growing like wildfire.

"But it's not just Minneapolis, because, well, you know what people've been reading over the past few months. *IPA, PAR,*[1]*Accounting Today, Practical Accountant*—everybody reads those publications, and you know what last year's figures were, that they reported. The CPA profession had its best growth year since the late '90s, but Crandall & Potter did not."

Displaying the kind of sure-handed knowledge Joe had grown to expect from Eric, the younger man ticked off the alarming details. "Aggregate growth for the top one hundred firms of more than sixteen percent; many firms growing at well over twenty. Compared to us—we grew just seven percent last year!

"So at first it was just a couple of people talking, but then they started asking around, checking with their friends. And it sort of took on a life of its own.

"And you know how it is, there's grumbling about one subject, and then pretty soon there's something else that's wrong. And I do think, in all honesty, that in some ways they have a point. We aren't experiencing the kind of growth we could. But somehow, the problem's being simplified, and it's become *you*, Joe. As managing partner of the firm, you're responsible for everything, so that means you're responsible for this too."

"Specifics?" Joe asked.

"Well, everybody's got their own ax to grind. Harold, he's been threatening to retire the whole time I've been here. Well, now he's finally close enough to read the writing on the gold watch, and he doesn't like what it says. He's seen all these growth numbers floating around, and he's thinking his share of the Crandall & Potter pie isn't worth what it should be, because the pie itself should be bigger."

Eric tapped another finger as he went through the list in his head. "Kevin," he continued. "Kevin's beef, best that I can make it out, is that he's carrying his load, he's doing his share to bring in business, and what

---

[1]*Inside Public Accounting, Public Accounting Report.*

is everybody else contributing? 'I make rain; everybody should make rain!'" Eric imitated Kevin, pumping his arm and speaking in an exaggerated tone.

"Even Charles chipped in yesterday afternoon," Eric finished. "There were a couple of guys kicking around the new auditing standards that just came out, and the talk started up again. And Charles had to toss in his two cents' worth."

Joe's eyes narrowed in surprise. "Charles?"

"Yeah, I know. Charles doesn't even bother to notice the rest of us unless he has a gripe. Well, he's got one now. He was kind of light on the details, but his point seemed to be that we missed the boat on 404 work, and again, somehow, that's your fault."

Joe slapped his desk in frustration. "That was in *his* bailiwick—404! I asked him about it a long time ago, even pressed him on it, and he blew it off completely. Said we 'didn't need to go there.'"

"Well," Eric said, "he wishes we'd gone there now. Maybe he was just piling on, but . . . " His voice trailed off.

"The thing is, Joe, I do think they have a point—at least some of them do. This firm is not growing the way it should. The opportunities are there—hey, it's like a stampede, they're coming at us so fast—and we're just not grabbing on. We're not even *trying*. We sit around doing the same old things, chasing leads the same old way, and making the same old excuses when we lose out.

"How are the other firms doing it? How are they racking up those kinds of gains? Do you have any idea?"

"Do *You* See It, Joe?"

Joe took a deep breath. As a matter of fact, he did have a pretty good idea what some other firms were doing. He'd attended an association meeting in June, and the whole focus of the meeting was disciplined growth and how to achieve it. A few key phrases floated back: best practices, disciplined growth, pipelines, revenue segmentation, product management.

Joe stirred in his chair. "Well, a number of ways, I guess. There are some new kinds of business available today, that's true. And some firms are going after them very aggressively. But that's not the way we do things here at Crandall & Potter. That's *never* been the way we do things."

He leaned forward to press his case. "And the way we do things is not half bad, Eric. All the partners here make a very good living. We're all in this together, we all work very hard, and everyone is more than comfortable—"

"Maybe we're a little too comfortable," Eric cut in. "Comfortable may not cut it anymore."

"Think about what you're saying, Eric! It's only been seven years since Old Man Potter died! That's the biggest transition this firm has ever gone through. I'm not sure we're ready for another major shake-up."

"Joe," Eric said, his voice trembling from the effort to speak as calmly, as persuasively, as he could, "I'm afraid you're not hearing me. This is not about whether or not people like each other, it's about business! Just look at the way things work around here. It's like all the partners are in cocoons; people barely talk to each other except to shoot the breeze. There's no rhyme or reason to our business development efforts—it's just not there. Tiff finally got the new brochure done, and it's a beauty, but there has to be more to marketing than that. And Ty. How much have we gotten out of Ty over the last twelve months?"

Joe started to say something in defense of Tiff Hollister and Ty Dukes, their marketing director and business developer, but Eric was on a roll. "Still, that's just staff, and the weight should really be on the partners' shoulders. So let's look at how our partners go about their business. First, every partner feels like he's in business for himself, so we compete against each other for clients and sometimes one partner will lock another one out of an opportunity—just to maintain control!

"There's no effective division of labor or delegation of work to junior members of the firm, so partners end up doing work like 1040s—which is a complete waste of their time—and, again, why? Just so they can maintain control over 'their' clients.

"What else does that mean? Well, for one thing, it means junior managers aren't brought along properly, aren't groomed and given increasing responsibility under the right kind of supervision.

"That's bad enough for the younger people, but from a productivity standpoint, it's disastrous for the partners. First, since they're spending so much time doing low-level work, they don't have time or energy to look for new business.

"And where *does* their energy go? To screaming bloody murder whenever anybody suggests that there might be a better way to do it. Remember when I proposed setting up a dedicated 'tax center' to do 1040 work? You'd have thought I'd suggested cutting off their right arms! They wouldn't even consider the idea of giving up this boring, tedious work that nobody really enjoys anyway. Why? Because these are 'their' clients we're talking about, and they're determined to hold onto every client they have with both hands!"

Joe raised a hand to interrupt, but Eric wasn't done yet. "So that's what they *are* doing, Joe, but let's talk for a minute about what they're *not*. First, they're not lifting a finger to cooperate with any marketing initiatives, and in fact the only time they stoop to acknowledge marketing is when they're throwing spitballs at it. There are some things Tiff can do, and I think she's trying to do them, but she gets basically zero help or backup from most of the partners.

"She runs an event, and they can't be bothered to follow up on the leads it generates. She sends out a letter about a tax law change, and they won't even pick up the phone to make follow-up calls. No wonder we don't get much new business!

"And it's the same thing with Ty. I'll grant you that he hasn't been a barnburner, but what chance has he had, really? The partners treat him worse than Tiff, and that's saying something. Whenever they get a good lead, they shove Ty aside as 'inconsequential.' Then, when it's time to follow up on that opportunity, they let it fall to the side because they're too 'busy.' Ty wouldn't have been too busy—it's his job!— but he's long gone from the picture by this time. And then, big surprise, some other firm gets the business. This happens over and over and over again, and the pattern never changes.

"What are we good at? Well, we're pretty good at meetings. We have meeting after meeting—hey, we get together every two or three weeks—but what do we talk about when we meet? We debate endlessly about nothing!—about which color carpet to buy, or whether to change the office hours, or how many different kinds of coffee to provide. And we can't even agree on those things!

"Nothing gets decided, or if it does, it takes forever. And you spend your time playing politician, soothing everybody's ruffled feathers about whatever's bothering them this week. It's like you're managing a major league baseball team loaded with prima donna free agents. But we are a *team*, or we're supposed to be. We should be working together toward a single goal: serving our clients and developing new ones. But that particular model is completely lacking here.

"It doesn't have to be that way, though. Do you know how things work at my friend Brian's firm? They have meetings every other week—same as us, pretty much—but in *their* meetings, they don't spend time arguing about minutiae. They go over every single lead they're chasing, and everybody pools information. They work to bring all the available information together, they develop strategy and then refine it as they go along, and they keep the focus *constantly* on competition and how to win. They only chase promising leads, and when they decide which partner gets to pursue a particular lead, it goes to the partner who's best qualified, not the one who happened to be lucky enough to pick up the phone when the call came in.

"Also unlike us," Eric went on, "they don't waste time writing fifty-page proposals. Instead, they use that time talking to prospects, finding out about their specific needs, so the firm can figure out how to meet them. So that process actually becomes a means of trading information and building trust with prospects. They have a *disciplined* approach to pursuing leads; there's nothing at all haphazard about it."

Joe started to speak once more, but Eric again held up a hand. "I'm almost done; just let me finish this thought."

Eric took a deep breath. "Finally, when clients do come onboard, they don't 'belong' to any partner, they belong to the firm.

"And that's about it.

"So, as I said, that firm has a *plan*, they have a *strategy*, and it works.

"Do you see anything like that happening here?"

"What do you want me to say, Eric?" Joe asked, pushing back from his desk and standing. "You say—the *partners* say—they want changes, but I tried to get this bunch to make changes once, remember? I told them I wanted to give up my book of business to manage the firm full time. They said no, remember?"

"Maybe that change is part of the answer," Eric replied evenly. "But it can't be all of it, because it doesn't address all the problems. What we have here is a bunch of guys who basically do two things. They either hunker down in their offices filling out low-level tax returns, or they run around playing golf and chasing off to lunches that lead nowhere.

"In fact, I'm afraid that's a pretty good description of Crandall & Potter these days: We're a firm that's going nowhere. We're like a bunch of dinosaurs, or Neanderthals. We know how the game was played when everybody used spears and stones. But we don't know how to use modern methods—we don't even know what they are!

"The proof is in the pudding, and seven-percent growth is less than half the average for this profession last year. In other words, Joe, Crandall & Potter is more than fifty percent *below* the average!

"And I don't know all the answers, though I'll bet I could find some out easily enough. That's your job, though I'm not sure you really see it. Kevin and Harold and Charles—all those guys—may be out in left field on the details, but they're right on target about the need for change. And you're our best chance for making those changes. In a sense, whether everybody else knows it or not, we're all banking on you.

"But the question is, Do *you* see it, Joe? Do *you* see the need for change? Do you see the headlights bearing down on this firm? Do you see what's ahead for us if we *don't* make changes, starting now?"

How Did This Happen to Me?!?

Eric stood quietly and slipped from the room. Joe sat for a moment, lost in thought. Then he stood, grabbed his keys and coat, and made his way from the building. Two partners started to greet him as he strode toward the rear exit, but a second glance at his face led them to change their comments to nods.

Joe failed even to acknowledge the nods. He was lost in his own thoughts, his own troubled world.

Joe maneuvered his black Mercedes E550 sedan out of the firm parking lot and guided it through the busy streets toward I-94. He pulled into the stream of traffic, pointed his car toward Wisconsin, and tried to think.

Where to start?

It began with Old Man Potter, Joe supposed. Potter, one of the two founding members of Crandall & Potter, had taken over as managing partner after the firm was only a few years old, when Crandall, 15 years his senior, had retired. Harold Brumlow, today the eldest partner at C&P, was also a holdover from the firm's earliest days. He'd been Old Man Potter's contemporary in age but not vision, so Old Man Potter had had to build *around* Harold rather than *with* him.

Potter had chosen Joe, first as a newly minted accountant, fresh out of school, and then, in time, as his successor, the one selected to carry on his dream. Joe had always felt that responsibility keenly, and the possibility that he might be discharging it poorly weighed heavily on him now. What's more, he had brought Eric along in just the same way, believing Eric would take over as managing partner someday. Not anytime soon, of course, for Joe had only been sitting in the MP's chair for seven years, and Eric was still too young for the others to take seriously. But that had been his plan—for Eric to inherit his managing partner's seat.

How ironic, then, that it was Eric coming to bring the message that the rules had changed, that the game itself had changed, that he might have to give up the chair himself, and not altogether voluntarily.

Joe tried to weigh the options realistically. First was the option of engineering a merger with a larger firm. Because change, God knows, was not easy or cheap, and were the C&P partners really ready for it?

Think of the investment they'll have to make! Joe thought. Think about the negative hit that would mean, for both the bottom line and the partners' wallets. Think of the uncertainty, and the enormous potential for failure.

Failure! Joe had never failed in his life, and he felt fear stirring within him. What would he do—he, Joe Abriola, a 55-year-old man with a wife and three kids—if he left Crandall & Potter? This firm was his life!

What would the rest of the partners do? Had any of them ever given a thought to a Plan B, or had they all simply assumed, as he had, that C&P would roll merrily and uneventfully into the future? Joe's experience suggested that they'd all pictured the future pretty much the way he had—they would all "get out there" and "do good work"; after all, wasn't that Old Man Potter's prescription for success?—and the good results would follow, and the growth would follow, and success would follow.

Well. That's what they'd been doing all these years, and what they were facing today hardly felt like success.

So when *did* the rules change? he wondered. When did the "good old ways" fade into irrelevance? Joe knew there could only be one answer: It had crept up while they weren't looking, while they were "getting out there" and "doing good work." In other words, while they were engaged in carrying out business as usual.

A white panel truck swerved into the lane just ahead of Joe, cutting it way too close and forcing him to stand on the brakes. *Good grief!* he thought. *Where'd that one come from?*

And as he signaled to exit from the highway and head back toward home, he allowed the weariness that had been worrying the base of his skull since the talk with Eric to come full front for the first time.

I really am very tired of all this, he admitted. And then the weight of every single partner and every staff member seemed to press down on his shoulders. *Why is it me who has to carry the whole burden?* he wondered. *Why am I the one who lies awake at night sweating about this stuff? Nobody else cares a whit.*

He also wasn't trained for this, he knew. Old Man Potter had chosen him largely because of his abilities as a mediator and conciliator, since in a firm with two dozen partners, egos can run riot, and a strong personality is needed to hold things together. Yes, that might be the best description of his key responsibility at Crandall & Potter, Joe admitted—holding things together, holding the partnership together, guarding the quality of the work product to protect the firm's reputation for excellence, keeping people happy and productive so the money continued to flow.

Joe's thoughts went back to his lack of training in the new way of doing business Eric had mentioned. He honestly didn't know if he had the skills to master it. Tugging steadily, inexorably, at the edge of his consciousness was a nagging feeling of doubt that seemed to drain the confidence right out of him.

Strip everything else away and it comes down to this, Joe thought. *Maybe Old Man Potter made a mistake. Maybe he picked the wrong guy.*

Then maybe he should just relinquish his position as managing partner and turn the firm over to somebody else. *And wouldn't that be heaven!*

The thought sprang unbidden to Joe's mind, startling him with its intensity. He allowed it to rest there for a moment as he picked at its edges, drawn to it yet just a bit afraid to touch.

He was surprised by how attractive the idea felt. Indeed, the prospect of shedding this mantle of responsibility seemed to act as a tonic on his bedraggled spirits. *To just have to show up every day and work with clients,* he thought wistfully, *and let somebody else worry about the big picture.*

As Joe contemplated this alluring notion, the next thing that stole over him was a keen disappointment that the partners showed so little appreciation of the leadership he'd demonstrated so far.

Given that, did it even make sense to try to push forward, if everyone was so dissatisfied?

What's more, Joe suspected that they would fight tooth and nail against any substantive changes. Look what happened two years ago, when he'd gone to the executive committee to propose giving up his book of business to focus full time on being MP. There'd nearly been an insurrection! You'd have thought he'd suggested dancing naked at the firm's holiday party.

The first part of that, Joe knew, was money. His paycheck was very little fatter each month from his MP duties, and the dab of extra money was nothing close to what the aggravation justified.

Sure, they'd told him, we'll take your book of business and split it up. But once you do that, there's no going back, no getting those clients back. The elephant in the room that had gone unmentioned, of course, was that if the partners should later decide they didn't need a full-time managing partner, he'd be out of luck, with no book of business to fall back on. *That's the way to show support for your leader!* Joe thought caustically.

There was another financial consideration as well. Since his retirement compensation was tied directly to three of the five best years of his earnings, how could he afford to give up his book of business if the partners weren't willing to protect him financially?

He couldn't, Joe realized, and that's what had caused him to abandon the effort before.

As Joe pulled into his driveway, he took the next step. *All right,* he thought, *if they don't want me as MP, then who should it be?* His shoulders sagged as he acknowledged almost instantly that there was no one else in the firm who was ready and able to assume the reins. Eric would be, in another five to seven years, but not now.

As he unlocked the door and stepped inside the house, Joe considered the notion that Potter had erred in choosing him as his successor. Maybe Potter should have just cashed out and sold the firm, rather than demonstrating such faith in Joe—a faith that suddenly seemed very suspect. Joe's thoughts drifted back to all the father-and-son talks they'd had over the years, and he felt a piercing sense of loss. Joe had looked up to Potter and respected him, counted on him for leadership.

But then Joe's memory forced forth a cold reality—that Potter's leadership, while stalwart, had also been firm and unbending. While his intent may have been benign, he'd been a very tough taskmaster. Joe tried to summon an image of Potter going to the partners to beg for authority to take the firm in a desperately needed new direction. Would he have stood still while they hung him out to dry?

No way.

Old Man Potter had succeeded in his own era because he'd been a leader, Joe realized, even when leading was difficult. How easy could it have been to build around Harold Brumlow, essentially passing him over for leadership as the firm grew? How easy was it for Potter to choose Joe when other partners might have coveted that senior spot?

And so it slowly dawned on Joe, with the gauze of sentimentality stripped away, that *he* had become Old Man Potter, that the solemn trust had devolved onto his shoulders.

I've been the guy out front, Joe realized, *but I've never been a* leader. *With all that I've done and left undone at this firm, I could never be called a leader.* And then Eric's words came back, clear and unflinching: "You're our best chance. . . . We're all banking on you." Joe knew he had a profound responsibility, both to the firm and to Old Man Potter's memory. He also knew that if he failed, it was all but inevitable that the firm would be swallowed up.

And so he took the next step, feeling calm and right in doing so. *This is my firm and my responsibility,* Joe said, pronouncing the words aloud to deepen his resolve. *I want to lead. I can lead. And I will.*

What Would Old Man Potter Do?

So how to proceed? First, Joe wondered about the advice Old Man Potter might give, were he to stage a miraculous reappearance at Joe's side for a quick confab. Joe remembered Potter's guiding principle, which was simplicity itself. "It's all about the client," Potter had preached. "Do good client work and the rest will take care of itself." *Well,* Joe thought, *that was then and this is now. No help there.*

Well, then, what kind of general approach might Potter suggest? Joe guessed that that discussion would start with a rundown of the rogues' gallery of current C&P partners. Who might have something useful to contribute?

Eric—Joe smiled fondly—ah, yes, Eric was clearly the class of the outfit. He was a niche rainmaker, the best Joe had seen in a long, long time. He'd come to C&P from a larger firm where he'd already received good rainmaking training (Joe called it "good potty training"). Today, he had all three of the skills—rainmaking, delivery, and management—necessary to make a niche grow. What's more, Eric was a born leader, organized, with terrific interpersonal skills. Finally, he was unique among his peers in possessing a real willingness to think in new ways. Though he was clearly a few years away from taking over, Eric undoubtedly represented the future of Crandall & Potter.

Next up, Harold. Joe sighed and then, suddenly, chuckled, as he seemed to feel the spirit of Old Man Potter brushing against his shoulder. How many evenings he and the old man had spent together, drinks in hand, kicking Harold—well, the subject of Harold—around! Perhaps because he was the first professional Crandall and Potter had taken on in their fledgling firm, Harold enjoyed something like protected status—fossil status, you might call it—at C&P.

He was perfectly consistent. He didn't ever want to retire, he didn't ever want to work hard, he didn't ever want to innovate. What a combination! Harold's nickname within the firm was RIP, for Retired in Place—or, in a variation Joe had heard more than a few times, Rest in Peace. (Joe personally favored a third version that had also made the rounds: Rip Van Winkle.) That's how much relevance Harold had in the firm's day-to-day operations.

But when the buyout of Old Man Potter's shares had been completed upon his retirement seven years ago, Harold had found himself in the enviable position of owning the largest single block of shares in the firm. It was that and that alone that had protected him from being marginalized completely.

There was also a rumor—Joe had heard the stories—that Harold used to enjoy some actual technical prowess. Isn't that why Potter chose him in the first place? But then Potter discovered, too late, that Harold could never get his head out of the general ledger, and there went his chance to inherit leadership of the firm.

Still, Joe knew that even though Harold's skills were now modest at best, he retained a lot of clout. *And he's found a way to turn his looming retirement into a problem,* Joe thought. *Interesting.*

But is there any help there? Joe asked himself the question and answered it simultaneously. Fat chance! He stifled a guffaw. First, Harold was jaded and negative, and even though he seemed to think he'd seen it all and knew all the answers, none of that wisdom ever managed to get passed along to others. What *did* get passed along were his caustic comments when things failed to work out as expected.

More than anything, though, it was his relentless insistence on throwing cold water on everybody else's enthusiasm that bled the energy from anything he was involved with. Joe had seen that happen far too many times, seen Harold destroy projects by his very presence. No, Harold was not likely to furnish any part of a solution.

Okay, Kevin McCoy, the resident tax guru. The consummate deal guy, but Joe had noticed that it was small to midsize transactions only. Had Kevin ever landed a really big fish? Joe racked his brain. Not that he could recall; Kevin seemed content to reside at the low end of the market.

What Kevin loved was people. He loved taking them to lunch, loved saving them money on their taxes, loved getting slapped on the back for doing so. At 43 years of age, it seemed like he spent a third of his time at the country club . . . but shouldn't there be some really well-heeled guys at the country club? If so, Kevin apparently hadn't run into them yet.

What's more, he was tremendously disorganized and refused to stick to any firm rules. Still, he did bring money in consistently—a fair amount of money, in small and medium-size chunks—and now he thought he was doing more than his share. Joe felt annoyed, but decided to set those feelings aside to devote his attention to yet another partner.

Charles Krueger. Now, there was a story—the auditor's auditor, a meticulous man who'd raised the audit to an art form. Joe knew Charles to be a workaholic loner who viewed marketing as a load of hogwash and didn't care if he ever got along with anyone. Charles routinely worked 80 hours a week and—the polar opposite of Kevin—never went out for lunch.

In fact, Joe had heard managers laugh that Charles was "burrowed up in his office like an armadillo," an underling trained to "toss a sandwich into his lair" from time to time. That's all Charles needed, and he was happy as could be. (In fact, lunch was his secretary's responsibility; she ran out to get him a sandwich when he bellowed at her each afternoon.) Lunch with a client was a foreign concept.

Charles had shown zero interest in participating in the firm's leadership, yet he was on the executive committee—along with Kevin and Eric—because the other partners trusted his auditing prowess to keep them out of lawsuits.

But Charles was problematic in so many ways, the most damaging his utter refusal to take ownership. Joe's mind slipped back to the afternoon's uncomfortable meeting with Eric, and he chafed at the memory of Charles's comments about 404 work slipping by. Joe knew the firm had missed the 404 bubble *because* of Charles, since he himself had broached the subject with Charles, only to be rebuffed. He vividly recalled Charles telling him, "Listen, we just don't have the talent," then bending his head back rudely into the work papers on his desk.

So what? *Nobody* had the talent in that field back then! Other firms had obviously found a way to figure it out.

Even within Charles's own specialty, Joe knew things had gotten out of hand. People had bowed down to Charles, because of his technical prowess, for so long that he was essentially answerable to no one. What's more, Joe knew of two opportunities the firm had lost in the last six months alone, where C&P's pricing was 25 percent higher than all the other competitors'. He was convinced it was because Charles had overdesigned the work. Charles had gotten away with it, to this point, by using the spectre of potential lawsuits to scare people into going along with his proposals. But Joe knew other firms had the same concerns about lawsuits, and they managed to cover that contingency without pricing themselves out of opportunities.

The fact of the matter was that Charles was pricing things too high because his audits were such works of art. *I think he's forgotten,* Joe reflected, *that we're in business to make money!*

The Usual Suspects

Who's left? Joe wondered, and his thoughts turned to Jackie Brown, the firm's very capable chief operating officer; Tiff Hollister, their marketing director; and Ty Dukes, the resident gladhander.

Now, isn't that an interesting description? Joe thought. He knew how little respect Ty commanded among the partners, and it bothered him. With characteristic honesty, Joe admitted that part of his concern came from the fact that he'd hired Ty, but it was more than that. When the partners in a firm refused to grant respect to the firm's business developer, that firm's business development effort was bound to suffer.

Joe mixed himself a Scotch and settled into his favorite chair, savoring this rare night alone in the house. Not that he didn't love his wife, but tonight's task called for quiet and focus. He intended to use the time wisely.

He took a moment to review the specific criticisms he'd heard about Ty. First, he drove a canary yellow vintage Corvette, and nobody could figure out where he'd gotten the money to pay for it. In the same vein, he sometimes sported a diamond pinkie ring—not a huge one, mind you, but a pinkie ring just the same.

What the devil, Joe thought, *I might as well be honest about it.* Somehow or other, Ty had picked up a reputation as a lady's man, and that was the wrong image for someone who represented an accounting firm. Joe had even heard a rumor that, if true, would be quite serious—that Ty had dated clients. There had never been any specific allegations, though, and Joe tended to chalk up the talk to frustration and pique. Joe simply couldn't believe Ty would be that indiscreet. Still, there was no question that Ty was very different from the partners, and that made him an easy target.

Joe winced as he recalled an exchange that had taken place before a meeting a couple of months ago. He didn't remember how it had started; probably it had already been under way when he'd walked into the room.

"Joe, how could you hire somebody who wears a pinkie ring?" Ben Spencer's eyes were twinkling, and the others—maybe half the partners were in the room already—were chuckling along with him.

Joe had been taken aback, he remembered, but he'd responded good naturedly, "I'm pretty sure he didn't have it on when he interviewed."

"Funny how he could have left out such an important item in his ensemble," Kevin McCoy chimed in. "He seems to have a real fondness for the thing. Have you noticed how he keeps that hand in motion constantly to make sure the diamonds catch the light?"

"Diamonds?" Harold Brumlow put in. "Where does he get the money?" Trust Harold to zero in on the dollars and cents, nothing more.

"Maybe from the high salary we're paying him," Eric had joked.

"Right!" someone else had cackled. "Fat chance! More likely it's cubic zirconium."

"Well, I've noticed he always wears it at two times," Kevin pointed out. "Every Thursday, and when he's got on a blue pinstriped suit. You think Thursday's a big night for Ty-Guy?"

"I think he picked it to match the Corvette," someone else put in.

Charles looked up from his papers for the first time. "Judith says she never trusts a man who wears a pinkie ring. She calls it the 'pinkie ring doctrine,' and she says it's infallible." Charles's eyes went back down to his papers immediately, his contribution to the conversation over. At the mention of Judith, though, the room fell briefly quiet. Some of the older partners remembered meeting the mysterious Judith—albeit briefly—at a holiday party many years ago. (In fact, one thought with a smile, it was *so* long ago that it was the *Christmas* party then!) The younger partners were scratching their heads, thinking, Judith? Who's Judith?

Kevin got the conversation going again. "I guess Ty didn't get that memo," he put in, chuckling. "He must think the ladies are charmed out of their nylon stockings by a pinkie ring."

At that point the first female voice entered the conversation, and every man at the table looked up. "Well, *I* was never charmed by a pinkie ring." Jackie Brown had entered the room, and without a hint of effort restored professionalism to a conversation that could easily have veered into the crude.

That's just like Jackie, Joe thought. Effective, effortlessly.

Jackie was a real success story at Crandall & Potter, and most people knew it. She ran a tight ship and managed to keep everyone in line without stepping on toes or wheedling. Not bad, especially for someone with no formal training. Jackie had come up through the ranks at C&P, having started as a secretary/receptionist when her husband walked out on her 20 years ago.

She'd made the most of every opportunity to learn and grow, and she now handled every important corporate function—human relations, IT, and finance—within Crandall & Potter. *How had she mastered IT?* Joe wondered. He didn't altogether understand it himself.

No matter. These days, Jackie was a fixture at C&P, and if you wanted to turn every single partner into a nervous wreck overnight, Joe thought, just tell them Jackie was thinking about moving on. Merely thinking it in jest sent a shiver of fear rippling up Joe's spine. *He* was the one who would blanch if she quit! Fortunately, Joe knew Jackie loved C&P as much as C&P loved her. She was a strong asset and could furnish critical support in the upcoming skirmishes.

In terms of key staff, that left only Tiff—Tiffany Hollister, a 31-year-old executive Joe had once heard called Brochure Babe by a fresh-mouthed younger partner.

Joe sighed, for he knew the implied criticism was not altogether un-fair. As befit a marketing director, Tiff was always upbeat, with a smile on her face, but she often came across as superficial. *Was* she a real lightweight? She was fond of saying she'd fallen in love with marketing in college, but accounting was a course she'd dropped because it was too . . . Well, take your pick. She'd told Joe in her interview, with a slight self-deprecating moue, that she'd found accounting boring. But Eric had confided that he'd heard Tiff and Ty—honestly, the two seemed inseparable sometimes; they even had a joint label, "Tiff'n'Ty"—laughing in the lunchroom one morning, and Tiff was talking about how *hard* accounting was, how she was so impressed that these people could sit around all day doing something she had found so incredibly *difficult.*

How much respect did she command from the partners? More than Ty, but not a whole lot more; Tiff was viewed more as an intellectual lightweight than a fool. Of course she picked up on that lack of respect and grew frustrated when she was left out of projects in which she had a legitimate stake. So things then came full circle—the partners, led by Charles, viewed her frustration as evidence that she really didn't deserve to be taken seriously—and on it went, round and round and round, unceasingly.

Joe had heard the complaints. "Isn't it part of her job to make the firm grow?" "What are we paying her for?" You couldn't really blame her, though, Joe thought, when people never really gave her a chance.

Joe's instincts told him that Tiff wanted to do the job well, but that she hadn't figured out how. Teaching her how . . . he supposed that would become his new job, or one of them. Still, Joe wondered, how was he supposed to teach Tiff how to take the lead in an area he didn't understand himself? He was a CPA, for crying out loud, not a marketer.

"Round up the usual suspects!" That was the command from on high in one of his favorite movies. This was his own group of "usual suspects"—his ragtag band of more senior partners plus three key staffers, of whom precisely one was clearly qualified for the job she held. Perhaps not the most promising group ever assembled, Joe allowed. But it would have to do.

Joe in the Snow

Joe sat wedged in the narrow seat, grateful at least that the Minneapolis-to-Philadelphia route was still traveled heavily enough to allow for full-size planes. Especially, he thought, since a freakishly early snowstorm had hit the Twin Cities that morning, and the plane had barely gotten off the ground before the cancellation notices started hitting the display monitors. He had to go through O'Hare, and that was a pain, but at least he didn't have to take off in a puddle-jumper during a snowstorm to go visit his friend.

Joe had met Alex Weinstein in June, at a meeting of the CPA Growth Alliance, an association of American and international CPA firms. They had hit it off over drinks in the bar, establishing an easy camaraderie with talk of college sports. Joe had played quarterback at Notre Dame (though not often; his top spot was third on the depth chart), and Alex had been on the lacrosse team at Pace University in New York City.

When the talk had turned, inevitably, to business, Joe had been astounded by the numbers Alex reported. Joe had limped into the meetings toting a measly 7-percent growth rate and felt blindsided to hear about growth rates among comparable firms in excess of 20 percent. Jeez, the *aggregate* for the top 100 CPA firms last year was above 16 percent—more than twice what Crandall & Potter had managed. Even more distressing was the fact that C&P had slipped out of the top 100 because of its lackluster growth rate.

What's more, Joe realized after looking at Crandall & Potter's latest growth numbers, most of his firm's 7-percent growth consisted of price increases, so in a sense it didn't really count.

Looking back, Joe found it remarkable that he had not felt an overpowering eagerness then to learn everything he possibly could.

He and Alex had compared notes, and Joe learned a little something about Weinstein & Federman, Alex's firm. Founded by Alex's father, Weinstein & Federman had puttered along, a sleepy firm with no real ambition, until Alex took over about 18 years ago.

What a trip! Alex had said. *Oy vey! The partners hardly knew what hit them!* Alex had started making changes immediately, and anyone who wasn't keen to get with the program was cordially invited to seek employment elsewhere.

His age at the time hadn't helped, either. Alex had been in his mid-30s, and there had been resistance to his authority, along with his plans.

It had worked, though—Alex had made it work. Some of the details blurred in Joe's memory, but he had no difficulty calling to mind the key figures: Weinstein & Federman was a $35-million firm with 20-percent-per-year sustained growth. Twenty percent a year on $35 million! Joe was deeply, profoundly impressed.

When talk had turned to Joe's own firm's performance, Joe's courage had faltered. Reluctant to own up to what suddenly felt like nearly criminal underperformance, he had sidestepped the question and told stories instead. He'd thought they were humorous tales shared by one MP with another, but he could tell by Alex's responses that he sensed problems behind the humor. Or maybe he just sensed my uneasiness, Joe told himself. He thought they'd both been more comfortable when they'd steered the conversation back to more casual topics.

There was no uneasiness when they swapped tales about kids and college choices, and they'd discovered that their personal backgrounds were quite similar, despite the obvious religious and ethnic differences. They'd chatted briefly a few more times during the conference, and when they'd left Chicago, Joe believed they both felt a solid bond of friendship.

Now Joe was on a plane, bound for Philadelphia. When he'd called Alex last Thursday afternoon, Alex had sounded glad to hear from him. He'd also seemed entirely unsurprised when Joe sketched out the situation.

"No problem, none at all," Alex had said. "In fact, your timing couldn't be better, if you can act fast—and I mean *really* fast. We've got a pipeline review slated for next Monday afternoon, and then Tuesday we'll have a segment leader meeting and a staff meeting. Do you think you could hop on a plane on Sunday?"

Well, of course he couldn't, and he'd said so at once. Hop on a plane? In three days' time? Obviously that was out of the question. "You know I can't do that," Joe had pointed out in a pained voice.

"Please think about it," Alex had replied in his friendly manner. "You've got a real problem on your hands; you said so yourself. If the future of your firm is what's at stake here, you can't reschedule a few meetings?"

"I don't know," Joe said. "When you put it that way . . . But—I don't do things that way. *We* don't do things that way! CPAs! You know that."

"I do know," Alex replied evenly. "I know that CPAs can be the most hidebound creatures on the face of the earth. But I also know something else. I know that flexibility can be an asset. As I said a minute ago, just take some time to think about it. While you're doing that, you might want to consider which meetings are more important to your firm's future—the meetings next week that you don't think you can postpone, or the meetings here that could show you a whole new way of doing business.

"Take some time, talk to your people, and see if you can't shift a few things around. Give me a call back if you can make it."

And so he'd dawdled and dithered and changed his mind five times in the space of three hours. Warring within him were two strong impulses. The first was convention. CPAs simply did not stop everything and jump on a plane at the drop of a hat! The second, though, was desperation. Joe had a natural fondness for the first priority, but as the day wore on he began to accept the inevitability of the second.

What choice did he have, really? His leadership effort at this firm was sinking, and his friend had offered to throw him a lifeline. He could ask Kevin to meet with the chemical company Monday morning, and Eric was already slated to lead Tuesday's discussion with the hospital administrators. Those were the two most important items, and everything else could be rescheduled easily enough.

So reluctantly, but with a sense of bowing to inexorable fate, Joe picked up the phone again just after five o'clock. "Can you come?" Alex asked when he picked up the call. "Can you see your way clear to get out here?"

Joe could and did. Now he found himself stuffed into his last-minute, cramped middle seat, nervous and uncomfortable, hurtling eastward through a blinding snowstorm, caught up in what could be the ride of his life.

Culture Shock

Joe sat alone in his hotel room Monday night and tried to collect his thoughts. Today had been an eye-opener. In fact, even that was a huge understatement. Closer to the truth would be this: Joe felt like he'd spent the entire afternoon getting hit between the eyes repeatedly by a two-by-four.

The resemblance between Weinstein & Federman and Crandall & Potter consisted of the following: They both called themselves CPA firms. That was it—beginning, middle, and end. It couldn't even be said that they both had managing partners, because he and Alex were both managing partners only in the sense that the guy who wrote "Three Blind Mice" was a composer alongside of Beethoven.

Joe rubbed his eyes and sighed. Then he grabbed his notebook and returned to the little table in the corner. He would try to jot down some more notes while things were fresh in his mind.

First, it was clear that Eric had been well informed about how well-disciplined firms developed and pursued leads. The pipeline review meeting today had been structured and streamlined. Every current opportunity was reviewed and every potential opportunity scrutinized during a withering general inspection.

Was this opportunity something in which the firm had expertise? If not, the "opportunity leader" was encouraged to rethink the strategy immediately, and the group moved on. (Eric's words about his friend Brian's firm came back to Joe: "They only chase promising leads. . . . ") W&F partners worked in teams, and people were assigned to leads based on criteria Crandall & Potter had never used—relationship skills, chemistry, and similarity in background between partner and prospect. (A new lead "goes to the partner who's best qualified.")

The revelations weren't confined to review of new leads, either. It was already clear to Joe that Alex's key staff—marketing, business development, and others—worked hand in glove with partners, respect extended and accepted on all sides.

Not everything he'd seen or heard today made sense to him, by a long shot. For instance, he'd heard several references to "divide and conquer," and there also seemed to be a heavy focus on "communications vehicles."

Perhaps most important of all, at no time during the entire afternoon had Joe ever gotten a whiff of anything even remotely resembling, "That's *my* client." He knew that at Crandall & Potter, they wouldn't be able to hold a five-minute meeting without that claim elbowing its way into the picture—prominently.

This is a wholly different beast, Joe thought, *and I had no clue that such a thing existed.*

He sat for a minute trying to imagine his own partners in this scenario. After a few minutes, he gave up. No matter how fiercely he tried, he simply could not fold Charles and Kevin and Harold—good heavens, Harold!—into the scenario he'd witnessed this afternoon. His imagination simply would not cooperate. It was like trying to imagine a Pop Warner team playing in the Super Bowl.

Indigestion for Breakfast

Tuesday evening found Joe back in his room again, alone, with a head that was all but spinning from the day's activities.

He and Alex had gotten a "running start," at Alex's suggestion, by meeting for breakfast that morning. Joe led off the discussion by regaling Alex with his attempts to imagine his partners behaving this way.

"It's a farce," he'd complained. "Your people are so focused, so motivated. They're committed, and committed *together*, to the same things—you can see it in their eyes even if you couldn't hear it in their voices, or understand one word coming out of their mouths. They are completely, one-hundred-percent different from my group.

"So how am I supposed to compete successfully with a group of second-rate partners?"

Alex had thrown back his head and laughed, that deep, hearty laugh Joe had found so appealing in Chicago. "And you think they were born that way?"

What had transpired was a mini-lecture from Alex on professional growth. "I do this full time, Joe. It's my job, ten hours a day, five days a week. My job is the partners. I'm their coach, their mentor. And that's *now*, when they're already there in terms of skills and attitude. I'm always fine-tuning the engine, day to day.

"When we started, though, believe me, you couldn't tell my people from yours. Here's how it went: Everybody had their own territory staked out. Everybody hid their best leads. Nobody told anybody anything, and nobody ever helped anybody else. It was each man for himself, and the devil take the hindmost."

That description sounded disturbingly familiar, and Joe said so.

"I know," Alex replied crisply. "It's *always* the same story. You remember the old saw from Tolstoy—that all happy families are alike, while the unhappy ones are unhappy in different ways?"

Joe had a vague recollection, but it was some years since he'd troubled to read Tolstoy, so he merely nodded.

"Well, I think he got it wrong. I think it's the *unhappy* families who are alike. They all do the same things. They hide their toys, and they won't share. They keep secrets, and they snipe at each other when their backs are turned. And if—no, not if, *when*—things turn out poorly, they practically tear a muscle pointing fingers at each other. When you have an underperforming group, it always works that way.

"I've spent the last several years helping a number of guys like you, Joe, and, believe me, the stories I hear are always pretty much the same. Your group's no different."

Alex gave Joe a moment to digest that, then went on. "Tell me, when we were at that meeting last summer, you heard a lot of this stuff being discussed, right? What was your reaction then? Did you decide to move on anything you heard?"

Joe hung his head for a moment, then lifted his chin and spoke. "No, I didn't," he said. "Instead, I suppose I made excuses. The general numbers that were bandied about, well, they were just aggregates, they didn't represent any actual firm.

"Then you and I talked, and, okay, here was a real firm that was growing like wildfire. I suppose I thought of ways to make your firm seem different. I remember thinking that Minneapolis is a much smaller market than Philadelphia." Joe paused for a moment, but Alex remained silent. "Another difference was that, since you're in Philly, with all those universities, your recruitment effort isn't always starved for young blood the way ours is."

"And you saw no growth figures for Minneapolis firms?"

Joe's face began to redden, but he knew Alex intended no malice, so he forced himself to continue speaking honestly. "No. I did. After the big Enron convictions, the *Minneapolis/St. Paul Business Journal* ran a story about Sarbanes-Oxley and the changes in the profession. The information was there—three local firms with high double-digit growth. One a tad above twenty, I think. I saw it. I was probably amazed by it. But I'm ashamed to say that I never looked into it, never asked myself or anybody else what the difference was between those firms and ours. I didn't ask." Joe lifted his hands and turned up his palms, then folded them on the table and looked down at them.

"I didn't ask," he repeated.

After breakfast, Alex and Joe had driven to Alex's office, and Alex had immediately introduced Joe to his right-hand person, Katherine Witt. Katherine's title was director of practice growth: "But don't let that fool you," Alex had said in Katherine's presence. "She does everything. She's amazing. She handles the business development function, too, and does both jobs magnificently."

Katherine had laughed, shaking hands, and said, "Believe everything Alex tells you."

Joe sat in on two meetings on Tuesday, a segment leader meeting and later a staff meeting. His head reeled as he continued to take in this utterly new approach. He noticed that the Weinstein & Federman group was broken down into teams, and that everything was designed to support those teams.

He began to get a sense of what "divide and conquer"—that phrase that kept popping up yesterday—actually meant, and then Alex spelled it out at lunch. "When you're developing an opportunity," Alex explained, "you divide the decision makers up and assign people to develop relationships with each of them one on one. Divide and conquer." Joe nodded in appreciation.

"It's something CPAs don't do instinctively, so you have to reinforce it constantly. But it's crucial, because it works."

Throughout both meetings, Joe marveled at the extent to which W&F partners took responsibility and ownership. And Katherine, in her capacity as business developer, was clearly an integral part of all efforts involving significant opportunities with both current clients and prospects.

At the staff meeting, Joe watched in amazement as various matters were discussed and resolved. Decisions were made! Real decisions! Substantive decisions! Decisions were *not* made at Crandall & Potter; instead, matters were tabled. But they don't table things here, Joe observed—even the messy, difficult things. They dive in and wrestle messy problems to a conclusion.

Finally, Joe was surprised at the level of give and take, at the openness of partners and their willingness to share seemingly everything they knew with the others. He could not in his wildest dreams imagine such a free and open exchange taking place at Crandall & Potter.

In fact, as the afternoon wore on, Joe found his thoughts focusing more and more on increasingly unflattering comparisons between the two firms, the two sets of partners and key staff. Where staff was concerned—in this case, Katherine Witt versus Tiff and Ty—there frankly wasn't much to compare. Tiff and Ty together couldn't hold a candle to Katherine. In fact, the very idea of such a comparison felt ludicrous.

Where the partners were concerned, Joe again found his group on the light side of the scale, even taking into account what Alex had said at breakfast. The partners Alex had assembled seemed focused and committed in a way he could not envision with his own group. He thought again briefly of the partners who sat on his executive committee—Eric, Kevin, and Charles—and compared them to Alex's management committee.

Even the best of his bunch, Eric, was mostly potential—a diamond in the rough. Kevin suddenly seemed like very small potatoes. Joe racked his brain, allowing his attention to wander from the meeting, in an effort to call up one single major opportunity that Kevin had ever even chased, let alone won. No. He couldn't think of a one.

Last, Charles—and at the thought of Charles, a sigh escaped from Joe's lips that was audible enough to draw glances from people seated near him. *How can I have a guy on my executive committee who's completely uninterested in being a leader in the firm?* Joe wondered. *How can I have a guy on my executive committee who isn't willing to work with anybody?*

The answer that always came back—that Charles provided a security blanket where potential lawsuits were concerned—just didn't seem to cut it any longer as justification.

Joe sensed that his thoughts had started down a dangerous path. *I don't need to think about this stuff now,* he thought. *I'm here to listen to Alex's people, not to obsess about my own.*

Joe did just that. He listened. For the rest of the afternoon, he listened.

A Toast to Hope

By the end of the day, Joe had a ton of notes and a heart full of hurt. He felt as if his own firm, Crandall & Potter, a respected name in the Minneapolis business community for nearly 50 years, had been exposed as a pretender. Even Old Man Potter, who normally was regarded with a respect bordering on reverence, was coming in for some licks.

After all, Potter had thought—and preached—that the sum of all wisdom in seeking new business was contained in his maxim, "Do good client work, and the business will follow." *We should have been changing course long ago,* Joe realized. *Then we'd have been in position to take advantage of the wealth of opportunities Sarbanes-Oxley opened up.*

During dinner, Alex tried to draw Joe out on the subject of his plans. He offered, gently, to come to Minneapolis and facilitate a partner session, but Joe declined the offer.

"Alex, I've learned so much here," Joe said. "I really feel like I've got a solid grasp on the essentials. I'm going to go back home, put together a plan of attack—schedule a pipeline review, start thinking about our annual retreat, which is coming up in about a month—and go from there. I think I can do it."

Alex smiled enigmatically. "Let's hope so," he said. He leaned back from the table. "You know, when I started this process at Weinstein, I needed some serious help. My executive committee was a mess, and my staff was very limited in the way they approached their jobs. My father held onto the MP position for a long time despite his age. He'd let things drag along in the old patterns for so long that everybody felt entrenched, even though the patterns were all dysfunctional."

"That's the way it is with us too," Joe replied. "Al Potter put together a pretty good group of CPAs, but it's not a group of people who work well together. Guys do the work that's on their desk, and they think it's pretty much up to a few rainmakers to bring in new clients. Just about everything that got talked about today is an area in which I'd have to say we've got problems."

Alex picked up his glass, took a long look at the light dancing off the brown liquid, and replied very carefully. "You still think you can take it on single-handedly, then. You think you can slay this beast."

"I do think so, Alex," Joe replied earnestly. "It may be a mess, but it's *my* mess, and I want to see if I can find a way out myself. You've shown me how to do it—in these meetings, and with the materials you've given me to take home."

Alex sat for a moment, then shook his head slightly. "Joe, I need to be honest with you," he said. He paused for a moment, and Joe nodded. "I've seen a couple of people try this alone, on their own. What happens—no matter how much preparation they do or how diligently they work to replicate methods that've succeeded elsewhere—they end up spinning their wheels. They just can't get it right on their own, no matter how hard they try."

"That's what you're saying?" Joe asked. "You're saying I'm not smart enough, or savvy enough, to carry it off? But *you* did."

"Not all on my own," Alex insisted. "I knew I needed help reforming my crew, so I went out looking for it. I knew of a guy—the older brother of a close college pal, a friend who had a key role in my wedding ceremony. Aaron's brother had a CPA firm that had just exploded with growth. I called Aaron, he called his brother David, and David met with me. And after he'd gotten to know me a little, he agreed to take me under his wing. I'll tell you, Joe, it was an *enormous* investment of time and energy on his part, and I'll be grateful to him till the day I die. If I gave you the impression that I did it all on my own, I certainly didn't mean to."

"And now you want to pass it along to me," Joe said thoughtfully.

"Well, that's not your only choice," Alex said. "There are also consulting firms that do exactly what I'd do—help you set things up in advance and then guide you through the process."

"I'd rather work with you than with someone I don't know," Joe said. "But I also have to be honest. I think I've learned a lot during this visit. And I think my partners will take this better if it comes from me rather than an outsider."

"Really," Alex said. "I've found the exact opposite to be true—that people won't listen to someone they know, but will pay attention to someone from the outside, especially if that person has a proven track record."

"You may be right," Joe said. "But I really do want to give it my best shot before I call in the cavalry."

Alex shrugged, Joe picked up his drink, and they touched glasses. "To the new regime at Crandall & Potter," Alex said.

"Hear, hear," Joe replied. His tone was fervent, but even more than that, it was hopeful.

Joe's Dreams . . . Joe's Mission

I need to turn in, Joe thought. *It's two more flights tomorrow, then I get to dig my car out of the parking lot at the airport.* But still he sat, glass in hand, allowing a few lingering thoughts to play out in his mind's eye.

More than anything, he kept wondering how he'd managed to ignore for so long the signs of change in his profession. There had been an onslaught of information, really, yet he'd managed to close his eyes to it all. *"Nose down to the grindstone, not up to the wind."* He sighed.

Other thoughts kept fighting for a foothold, and he finally relented. He allowed full rein to the frustration and jealousy—*there, might as well call things by their right names*—that he'd felt periodically throughout the day. He found himself comparing his accomplishments with Alex's. They'd both started out with roughly the same advantages. It's true that Alex had inherited his firm from his father, but Joe knew it was much smaller than Crandall & Potter when Alex had taken it over. The difference was Alex, and the changes Alex had made.

Alex had adapted, Joe knew, while he had not. He explored possible reasons for his own passivity and wondered why his posture had essentially been defensive. *Did I focus so much on survival—both for me and for the firm—that I grew blind to the possibility of seizing opportunities?*

As Joe continued down this melancholy path, his concerns grew broader. He thought about the priorities he had established during the last 20 to 30 years. Maybe they had been *de facto* priorities, but they counted all the same.

Where did those years go? Had he used them wisely? Thirty years ago, Joe remembered, he and his wife, Becky, were just starting out, she with the kids and he with his career. His major concerns then revolved around the basics: paying the bills, building a nest egg, putting aside some money for the kids' college. Now the youngest of their three was finally out of school—Vincent had gone to Notre Dame, like his old man—and all the old dreams had been forged into realities. Were there no new dreams to take their place?

I'll start with this, Joe thought, *and if it's not a dream, well, at least it's a mission—the need, and the willingness, to change and grow.*

Joe knew he held the seeds to success in his hand. During this two-day visit, he had witnessed a wealth of winning ideas in action: best practices, ways to achieve growth, the positive way in which peer pressure primes individuals' competitive juices in driving growth.

Joe then turned the harsh light of reality on himself and his partners and tried to achieve an honest assessment. Point One: He should have woken up and smelled the coffee in June, at the meeting in Chicago. He hadn't, and that was his failing.

Point Two: He was not a stupid man, nor even an especially obtuse one. There was more to what he'd heard in June than just the numbers. He'd grasped enough at that meeting to understand that significant growth came to firms that were willing to make sea changes in their ways of doing business.

Point Three: For a multitude of reasons, he'd believed instinctively that such changes were too sweeping to be practical at a hidebound institution like Crandall & Potter. What he'd heard described would require a huge commitment in both time and money from an executive committee that had slapped down his request for the wherewithal to function as a true managing partner. *For two years, I've been saying I need to give up my book of business and put myself on this full time,* he thought. Ruefully, he remembered the "offer" that had come back, that he was welcome to give up his book of business—with no guarantee that he could get it back if need be, and with no commitment to back his efforts as full-time MP.

So it's a structural problem, Joe concluded. *That means the only solution is to change the structure.*

The changes Joe had in mind would rock the foundations of Crandall & Potter more deeply than even he understood. Before it was over, many people would wonder if this sleepy Minneapolis accounting firm could withstand the strain.

And We're Off!

Joe sat at his desk, bright with expectation. Fifteen minutes from now, Crandall & Potter would hold its first-ever pipeline review meeting.

Working from sample forms Alex had given him, Joe had fashioned a brief e-mail message and circulated it immediately upon his return. It directed the partners, plus key staff, to gather all their "active opportunities," plus basic data about them, and forward the information to

Tiff. Further, everyone was directed to come to the meeting prepared to talk about these opportunities. Tiff had been tasked with assembling the opportunities and presenting them in comprehensive form for consideration at this historic first pipeline meeting.

Finally, Joe had directed Jackie Brown, the COO, to run segment numbers for the firm, to allow him to assess their current revenue breakdown by service line and industry. He'd given the job to Jackie immediately upon his return and expected to see the numbers shortly.

As the minutes ticked away toward 10 o'clock, Joe was aglow with anticipation. Change was finally under way at Crandall & Potter! The dinosaur was throwing off its scales at last!

What Joe had not been privy to was the reaction his message had elicited. Everyone knew he'd been to Philadelphia, and the general sense— confirmed when the e-mail message came out—was that he'd been off studying some new way to drum up business. Eric had worked hard to generate support for the forthcoming effort, but his enthusiasm had fallen on deaf ears.

When the message hit their inboxes, many partners simply hit delete after jotting down the date and time of the meeting. Others tossed the request to the side. They'd been through this kind of thing before. There had been attempts to streamline prospecting efforts in the past—hey, weren't they on their third business development person right now?— so a "new" approach was old hat to them. There had even been a joke going around in the lunchroom. Someone had made a comment about "soup du jour," and someone else cracked, " 'Pipeline review'—that's *program* du jour!"

Eric had stood tightlipped in the corner, then slipped from the room unnoticed. He wished Joe knew how things really stood with his "team"—but maybe he was better off not knowing. At any rate, it was too soon to go back to Joe with another "bad news" message.

At 10:20 a.m., Joe sat at the head of the conference table, dumbfounded and deflated. Once the meeting had begun, disillusionment had set in quickly.

On the positive side, all the partners had showed up for the meeting—well, everyone but Harold, and he hadn't graced them with his presence at a meeting in, what, five years or more? So that hardly qualified as a surprise. A little more than half the partners were physically present in the room, with the rest patched in by telephone. Tiff and Ty were there, with Tiff seated—rather nervously, it seemed to Joe—to his immediate right.

Joe opened the meeting by outlining the basic concept of a pipeline review. Working from Tiff's spreadsheet incorporating all the active opportunities that had been reported, they would discuss each opportunity individually. During his opening remarks, Joe moved his eyes around the table, hoping to receive nods of acknowledgment. Instead, he saw mostly noncommittal stares, mixed in with a few stifled yawns. Frank Pierce was already drumming his fingers on the table, making no effort to hide his disdain for the whole endeavor.

Joe asked Tiff to distribute the spreadsheet, and trouble set in at once. First, although there were 35 leads listed on the spreadsheet, Joe quickly calculated in his head that the dollar amounts totaled about 2 percent of C&P's annual revenues. In a firm of their size, Alex had told Joe to expect to see somewhere between 10 and 20 percent of annual revenues in the pipeline.

The second problem lay in the names that were attached to the opportunities. Everyone who had provided information to Tiff was included on the spreadsheet. But of the 24 partners at Crandall & Potter, only 8 names were listed.

Also noted beside each lead was the potential dollar amount for that opportunity, with the aggregate total for all opportunities recorded at the bottom of the column. And the addition was wrong! In a CPA firm, the marketing director—using a spreadsheet!—couldn't add up a list of numbers!

Joe felt a dull pain set in behind his eyes.

It was just the beginning.

Dream On, Joe!

It didn't take long for the addition problem to take center stage.

"Uh, Tiff, I think we've got a problem here with this total," Eric said.

"That's right," Ben Spencer chimed in. "There's way too much here to be . . . just under two hundred thousand? No. Let's see . . . "

Heads bent to the problem immediately, and Joe could sense Tiff stiffening in the seat next to his.

"Well, the first thing is," Eric began, "do we really have a lead for fifteen hundred and another for . . . two thousand?"

"Hah!" Frank's sarcastic chortle split the air.

Ignoring the outburst, Eric turned his eyes kindly toward Tiff. Red-faced, she refused to meet his gaze, keeping her eyes glued to the paper in front of her.

"Tiff, I think what must've happened," Matthew Hanover put in, "is that a long series of numbers got dropped somehow from the equation. This should be more like four hundred altogether." Matthew's voice was kind, too, and as always very earnest. At age 27 the youngest member of the firm, Matthew took everything seriously, and made no effort to hide it.

Unfortunately, not everyone was willing to overlook Tiff's mistake, and as Joe heard the snickers, he decided to move the discussion along.

"Yeah, it looks like about four hundred to me, too, so let's go from there.

"Actually, though," he added, "we have to back up, because there's lots of stuff missing here—or I certainly hope there is. Let's start with the fact that it looks like only eight people are on here." Joe turned to Tiff. "This sheet includes everybody's responses to my e-mail?"

"Yes," Tiff replied, "everyone who gave me information."

"*I'm* not on here," Ty pointed out.

"You're not a partner," Tiff blurted out, surprised enough by the tartness in her pal's voice to lift her red face from the spreadsheet.

"That doesn't mean I don't have leads." Ty sounded petulant, Joe thought—like a schoolboy who'd just found out his extra-credit project wouldn't count. "Ty *always* has leads," he insisted, frowning. "Ty has plenty of leads!"

"But you didn't get the e-mail."

"Yes, I did!"

By this point, Tiff had forgotten her earlier embarrassment, so intent was she on making sure she didn't get railroaded into taking the blame for another error. "Well, you didn't send anything back to me. You didn't send me *anything*! I know you didn't, because I've got all the responses right *here*!" With a flourish, Tiff pulled a slim manila folder from a stack and brandished it triumphantly.

"Of course I didn't," Ty replied. "Why would I send it to you? Ty has it all *right here*!" With an even bigger flourish, Ty produced his own document—a two-page, stapled spreadsheet, of which he seemed to have come equipped with a single copy.

"Let's take a look," Joe said, hoping to put a stop to the antics. Ty passed it over, then sat back, arms draped casually across his chest and a smug smile plastered firmly across his face.

Joe glanced at the paper, then forced a smile. "All right. Since this stuff is not on the master pipeline, we're going to need copies for everyone." He glanced over at his right-hand person with a smile. "Jackie?"

Jackie took the spreadsheet and moved into the hall to flag down an assistant. When she stepped back into the room, Joe still had the floor.

"Until those come back," he was saying, "let's get back to our main pipeline. All right. The first problem here is that we don't have everybody's input. So let's just go around the table. Tiff, you can take notes, and we'll add them to what we have already."

Joe started to speak again, then turned to Tiff, who was rising from her chair. "Tiff?" he asked.

"Well, I'm gonna go grab a calculator. If you want me to keep track."

"No, no," Joe said, "we can do this in our heads. Then you'll clean it up and print it out again later. Right now we just need to get the information out."

"If you're sure," Tiff said.

"Unbelievable!" Frank put in.

Joe could hear more snickers, so he turned quickly to his left. "Durwood, what've you got?"

As it happened, Durwood Poole had nothing, or so he said. Was that a surprise? Joe wondered, and he decided that it wasn't. Even for an elder partner known for his solid if unexceptional performance, having zero new business on the horizon qualified only as "What else is new?"

Sadly, Durwood wasn't the only one with no new irons in the fire.

"Smith?" Joe asked, when he'd gotten to Smith Smoot.

"Yes, I have several leads," Smith replied. "I guess I didn't send them to Tiff because, the problem was, well, I wasn't sure where to put them."

"Where to put them?" Joe echoed.

"On the sheet," Smith explained. "The attachment you sent. I wasn't sure if the leads I had were qualified or not."

"All right," Joe said. "That's fine. Let's get 'em out here and talk about them. We'll find out if they're qualified or not." Joe was hoping this would not turn treacherous. Smith Smoot was a good young accountant—a bit younger than Eric—and he'd made a real name for himself in the relatively new business valuation specialty. But despite his accomplishments, he could be maddeningly defensive about his work. On the other hand, Joe couldn't hold that against him too much. If he hadn't grown up saddled with a name like Smithton Smoot, who's to say how he'd've turned out?

"Well," Smith began, "I have three leads that I believe might be regarded as qualified. One is for a large dental practice. The founding dentist died, and the remaining dentists need to buy out his share from the widow. They need a business valuation done. So," Smith concluded, "I believe I would call that qualified."

"That sounds *possibly* qualified," Joe said carefully, pleased to be able to move into a teaching role. "A qualified lead would generally be one that incorporates both *need* and *potential*. That means their need is pressing enough that they *have to* make a decision, that they have the money to pay for our services, and, finally, that whoever you're talking to is authorized to make the decision. Does this opportunity fit that definition?"

"Yes, I think so," Smith replied, "because they have to value the business to buy out the widow . . . they're doing well financially . . . and there's one partner in place who's empowered to make the decision to hire us. That's need and potential.

"But, on the other hand," Smith went on after a brief pause, "there is some competition from a couple of other CPA firms, so it's not a done deal."

Durwood had looked as though he'd been napping, having apparently lost interest after making his personal report about nothing. At this point, however, he opened his eyes and leaned forward. "Joe, I'm a bit confused about 'qualified.'" Durwood stopped, as though uncertain of how to phrase his thoughts, and Matthew, who had developed a rapport with the older partner while assisting on some projects, stepped in smoothly to help.

"I had the same thought, Durwood. It's not like auditing, where a qualified opinion is not a good thing. It sounds as though, in business development, a qualified lead is *better* than an unqualified one.

"I have a couple of leads like that myself," Matthew went on. "So I'm not real clear—are they qualified or unqualified?"

"A couple of leads like *what*?" Joe asked. "We really need to slow down here, maybe back up and go over some definitions."

The dull ache behind Joe's eyes had turned into pounding, but he knew there was no choice but to forge ahead. "Let's start by looking at the categories . . . "

The next 10 minutes were devoted to studying and absorbing the differences between the two kinds of leads:

- Unqualified (Based on an initial discussion, the prospect might have a need.)
- Qualified (Discussion has clearly shown that they have both need and potential—that is, adequate "pain," the money to fix it, and a bona fide decision maker.)

"Now, are we all clear on that?" Joe asked finally, and, getting nods around the table, went on. "Okay, next let's talk about the status codes that are applied to opportunities." He outlined four possibilities:

1. Final (C&P is awaiting the prospect's approval)
2. Proposal (a proposal or engagement letter has been issued)
3. Qualified lead (based on the definition above)
4. Unqualified lead (based on the definition above)

"All clear?" Joe asked at last. "It's important—no, vital—that we're all on the same page about these pipeline components, because the pipeline is going to be a key part of our approach to every new opportunity from here on out."

"Well," Joshua Huberman asked, "where on the pipeline do I put a company we'd *like* to do business with?" Joe was mildly surprised that Josh had even asked a question. He was by far the quietest member of the firm—he made Charles look outgoing—and was also, frankly, the partner least likely to bring in leads of any type.

"Nowhere!" Ty pounced gleefully on the quiet man's error. "That's a *suspect*! And those don't belong on a pipeline, since there's no reason to believe they'd ever want to do business with *us*." He then added, with another frown, "Ty could explain all this to you, if you'd only ask."

Despite his distaste for Ty's antics, Joe had to endorse his statement. "That's true, Josh. Suspects are the stuff of pipe dreams, not pipelines."

With the definitions fleshed out, Joe hoped that they were all, at long last, on the same track.

Dream on, Joe!

Fancy Notepaper

After three partners in a row said they had no prospects to report, Joe decided to try a different approach. "Think of it this way," he said. "It's just . . . Who are you meeting with? What are you talking to people about?"

He took a deep breath. "With that in mind, we'll try again. You're next, Ben. What've you got in the fire?"

Fortunately, Ben Spencer had four leads, which brought the total number to 43. More than an hour later, the number stood at 49. Getting there, though, had been like pulling teeth.

Matthew had three leads, but getting the basic data on those three—name of company or organization, contact, current provider, and potential total revenue—involved sifting through more detail than anyone else at the table cared to endure. Smith Smoot, when all the concepts had been untangled, had three leads as well.

As the conversation picked up steam, the partners' enthusiasm had grown along with it, despite the occasional barbs lobbed out by Frank. People started making notes on Tiff's spreadsheet, then on notepads they'd brought along.

Durwood Poole had come emptyhanded, and he sat for a while affecting an air of supreme disinterest. Eventually, though, as the list grew, and the other partners continued to make notes and update the running totals, Durwood suddenly decided he felt left out. He shifted in his seat, then reached inside his coat pocket and found a pen. He reached down for his notepad and found himself without one.

He then stole a quick look around the table and decided it was safe. As unobtrusively as possible, he lifted his Starbucks cup slightly and slid the small brown napkin out. Glancing around rather than looking down, Durwood proceeded to unfold the napkin and spread it out into the largest surface it could provide. He then began jotting down a few notes of his own—taking care to press down very softly, to avoid tearing his "stationery."

Joe noticed it immediately and stared in horror, but then it suddenly struck him as funny. Durwood Poole, the third oldest partner in the august firm of Crandall & Potter, reduced to making notes on a Starbucks napkin. What a terrific metaphor for this entire bunch of partly interested, half-committed partners.

A Starbucks napkin, for heaven's sake!

Finally, someone else noticed. "Hey, nice letterhead, Durwood!" Jake Billings sang out. As heads turned in Durwood's direction, astonishment was followed by laughter.

"I didn't realize . . . " Durwood began, but he stopped when he realized where that thought was going. He hadn't known he'd need to take notes during a partners' meeting?

"Here," Eric said, ripping a section from his notepad. "One for all, and so forth, right?"

In a strange way, Durwood's gaffe seemed to unite the group in seriousness. Maybe this wasn't such a dumb idea after all.

"I Know the Controller!"

The count stood at 52 possible leads when the next rupture took place. Jake Billings had just announced a prospect—a general contractor specializing in medical office buildings—that had seemed solid a week ago but now appeared to be slipping away.

"Which firm, Jake?" Kevin called out. "Tiff has everything about this company but its *name*."

"Sorry," Jake said. "I thought I said that upfront. It's Medico Builders."

"Medico!" Kevin snapped. His jaw was clamped, and the veins stood out on his neck. "You're chasing Medico? And it's worth forty thousand? And you didn't tell me? My cousin is the controller for Medico, Jake! We could've waltzed right in the door!

"So where do we stand now? How far along are you? Who're we up against? Why do you think we're losing it? And *why the devil didn't you come ask me for help?*"

Jake leaned back in his chair and lifted his chin. "Why would I come to you about Medico, Kevin? It's not your area, it's construction."

"But he's my cousin!" Kevin insisted.

"And I'm supposed to know your whole family tree?"

Both men were getting hot under the collar, so Joe decided to intervene. "Hey, everybody, calm down. This is actually a good thing," he pointed out. "This is one big thing these pipeline reviews are designed to help with. By talking about our leads *together*, everybody learns what everybody else is working on, and if they can help out, they do. Otherwise, Jake, you're right, there's no way for you to know.

"And Kevin, you're right too, because you could probably have made a huge difference if you'd gotten involved with this one at the start. But it's not too late, and from now on, you two work together on Medico."

"That's right," Ty put in. "Working together—that's the key. That's what Ty's been trying to tell you guys for the last year. It's all about pipelines, and about coordinating our shots!"

Tiff could see that her friend's comments were not finding a positive reception, but apparently he could not. "And who's the *one guy* who's here for the *express purpose* of helping you win these things? It's *me*! Ty! You just have to come and ask!"

"Yes, Ty, that's certainly true," Joe cut in. From the look on Ty's face, it wasn't at all difficult to divine the words that might be on the verge of slipping out. Joe half-expected Ty's next comment to be "You guys have been stiff-arming Ty for a year! Maybe you'll listen now!" Since no earthly good could possibly come of such a declaration—and since Joe thought he might gag if he heard Ty refer to himself in the third person one more time today—Joe decided to change the subject by calling on another partner.

Perhaps consciously, perhaps unconsciously, Joe had called first on the partners from whom he had a reasonable expectation of leads. As he moved beyond those partners to others who had nothing to offer, the conversation began to degenerate.

Two partners, it turned out, were working on the same small consulting firm. "That firm has two consultants, and we're working—separately—with both?" Joe couldn't believe his ears. "We're competing against ourselves!?"

At the other end of the table, two partners started bickering about who had made the initial inroad with a company that represented one of the largest opportunities on the entire C&P slate. Joe tried to referee the discussion for a moment or two, then lost his patience.

"Stop the bickering, for Pete's sake!" he snapped. "The point is the business—not who brought it in the door."

He decided to make one more effort to pull the meeting back on track and get to the few partners who remained, before throwing in the towel—for today, at least.

Charles's Big Tuna

As he glanced at Tiff, who was bent studiously over her notes, Joe considered the partners' reactions to the information she was so diligently recording. Most seemed pleased to learn there was so much potential business they hadn't known about. Comments along the lines of "You're kidding! I didn't know we were working on that!" and "How did we get our foot in *that* door? That's terrific!" had been echoing about the room.

He wasn't sure when he wanted to drop the bomb—that even with all the potential business they had identified this morning, they were still miles away from where they should be.

Joe's thoughts were jerked back to the present when he heard Charles begin to speak. To Joe's tremendous annoyance, Charles had spent the entire meeting with his head propped on one hand, doodling—showing clear disdain, Joe felt, for the entire process. Apparently, though, Charles had decided that his moment had arrived, and when he spoke, his words provided the conversation stopper for the day.

"I suppose I've been remiss as well," he began. "I do have one opportunity in hand—in fact, *well* in hand, I believe. And I did fail to forward it to Tiffany for inclusion on her list."

"Okay," Tiff said, looking up from her notes. "Shoot."

Charles straightened in his chair, elbows on the table, fingertips steepled together. "We are close—quite close—to coming to terms on an audit and tax engagement."

It took a moment for Joe to realize that Charles was finished. "Yes?" he prompted.

"Yes, what?" Charles said.

"Well, tell us about it," Joe said in exasperation.

"Hmm, let's see." Charles considered for a moment. "It's Swanson Products." At those words, there was a collective intake of breath around the table. Charles had just named one of the largest companies in the central northeastern states, and there wasn't a person at the table who wasn't impressed. Oblivious to the reaction he'd elicited, Charles went on, "As I said, it is an audit and tax engagement. A banker acquaintance at First National told me about it a few weeks back. And . . . their board meets this week to make a decision."

This time it was Ty who got the sense that Charles was finished. Jackie's assistant had returned some time ago with the copies of his pipeline, and he grabbed a copy and opened his mouth to launch into that discussion, but Joe waved a hand sharply to cut him off.

"Just a minute," Joe said. "Charles, how large is the opportunity?" From Charles's casual demeanor, he didn't think it was significant, but with Charles, who ever knew? Anyway, they needed the information for the spreadsheet.

"Hmm, let me see . . . " Charles said, his voice trailing off as he began adding in his head. Lips pursed, he gazed sideways at the ceiling for a few moments, then turned his attention back to the others. "Altogether, I think, it's in the neighborhood of $350,000," he said, sounding for all the world as if he were talking about a *three*-thousand-dollar opportunity.

A stunned silence fell over the room, though again Charles didn't seem to notice. Then a few partners began to steal glances at each other, as the same thought raced like lightning from one mind to the next: *He doesn't get it. He really doesn't get it!*

It was far and away the largest opportunity in the pipeline, simply dwarfing all the rest. But to Charles, in his blindness, they were all the same.

There was complete silence for a full half minute, and Kevin was the one to break it. "No kidding," he said. "Tax and audit. And you were, maybe, going to tell the rest of us sometime? You were going to bring in the tax partner? Me?"

"I didn't need you, Kevin," Charles replied, displaying his special gift for choosing words that rankled. "It's under control. It's on the verge, the very verge, of being closed."

"Charles, something that big, something in tax work, you should have brought me in, let me have some input."

"Aren't you listening, Kevin? I didn't need your input. Sarah Brandeis"—a senior tax manager who handled the tax work for a number of Charles's audit clients—"worked up the estimate for the proposal, and you know she's competent on estimating jobs."

Kevin sat back, not at all mollified but resolving to let it go for now. As it happened, he agreed that Sarah was capable of handling that task. He was still outraged, though, that Charles had failed to show him the courtesy of at least informing him about the prospect. He made a mental note to discuss the situation with Sarah.

Joe stepped in. "All right. Tiff, let's add that to our list." *The understatement of the day,* Joe thought.

"Right," Tiff answered. "Swanson Products. Three hundred fifty thousand." She looked up at Charles. "Current provider?"

"Diggs & Carey," Charles responded.

"Contact there?"

"Probably Jim Diggs himself. I'm sure it's their biggest client."

Tiff glared across the table at Charles's smirk. "Very funny, Charles. Contact—*your* contact—at Swanson."

"Taylor DiStefano."

Joe leaned forward. "Let's fill in another cell on this one, Charles. If you look at Tiff's original spreadsheet—have you got that?" Charles didn't, but Ben Spencer, seated next to him, leaned over and shared his copy. "You'll see, near the left, there's a cell for 'most recent activity,' and then on the far right, there's another one for 'next step.' Fill us in on those, please."

"Very well," Charles said. "Most recent activity was last Friday. I was given to understand by Taylor that I'll hear by the end of this week, after their board meets. I suppose that satisfies both your cells, actually."

"Today's Wednesday," Joe pointed out. "When do you plan to follow up?"

"There's no reason to appear overanxious. I expect I'll get a call from Taylor any day now."

"I'd like to spend a few more minutes on this one, Charles, get a little better feel for it. This kind of opportunity is, needless to say, huge for a firm like ours. I'd feel more comfortable if I knew a little more about it—how it came about, why Swanson's leaving Diggs, how we got the inside track on it."

"Really, Joe, must we take up everyone's time on this? Let's do this: I'll stop in to see you later today. We'll go over all the specifics then."

Joe took a moment to consider. He really wanted more details— now—but he did not want to force a confrontation with Charles in the presence of all the partners. On balance, it was probably wiser to let it go for now.

"All right, Charles, I'll expect to see you later today to go over this in detail. For now, since Ty's list has been back here for some time"—Joe picked up the stack of copies and passed them around the table, feeling an optimism he hoped he was warranted—"let's find out what our business developer is bringing to the table."

Ty Lays an Egg

"So, Ty," Joe said. "Tell us what you've got."

As every eye turned to Ty, he leaned back sideways in his chair, arms draped casually to the side, a look of unbearable arrogance on his face. "Check," Ty said. "Given what we've seen so far, Joe, I think you'll find that Ty's right up there, in terms of leads."

Another teaching moment for the partner group, Joe thought. "The word 'lead' has a very specific meaning, as you know, Ty," he said. "So that's great. Let's take a look at them."

"There's a lot of stuff here," Jake Billings pointed out, with what sounded like awe in his voice. "What, looks like twenty or so in all."

"Twenty-one," Ty announced proudly.

As everyone took a moment to study Ty's "pipeline," a lead weight came to rest in the pit of Joe's stomach. Ty's list bore only a cursory resemblance to the document Alex used, the one Joe had mocked up for Tiff. Each listing contained the name of the prospect, a telephone number, and most but not all had a contact name. Most had a dollar amount, and some of the amounts were impressive—assuming the leads were legitimate. There were no dates, however, to reflect either past activity or future plans. And the category headed "Next step" was populated almost entirely with social engagements. The next move on all Ty's leads, it seems, was to feed them or entertain them.

"Okay," Joe said bravely. "Let's run through 'em. We'll start at the top with Wellington Brothers . . . "

Wellington Brothers, it transpired some time later, was the pinnacle of Ty's achievement for the day, and even it caused a bit of a ruckus. "Wellington Brothers! I knew there was somebody I forgot!"

Sixteen heads swiveled in unison toward Durwood Poole. "I knew there was a bona fide lead I was working! Yes, Wellington Brothers, Chad Jenkins. Played golf with him last month."

"Last month?" Ty said. "I met with Chad for breakfast last *week*, and he didn't say anything about playing golf with you."

"Don't know about that," Durwood replied. "I'll check my calendar, but I'm sure it was last month . . . unless it was, let me see, might have been a couple of months ago . . . " Durwood's voice trailed off as he trained his attention on the ceiling. Around the room, there were head shakes and shrugs. Everyone knew Durwood was a whiz with numbers, but he could otherwise be quite forgetful. It was altogether possible that the remembered golf date had taken place ages ago.

"Well, the point is, again, that the two of you didn't join forces," Joe observed. "So let's, one more time, look at this as a learning experience, and more underscoring of the reason for the pipeline.

"Ty, where does the Wellington effort stand?"

After a few minutes, it developed that there wasn't much of an effort of any kind under way with Wellington. Durwood had played golf, and Ty had had breakfast, and both were essentially social outings.

That set the tone, and 20 minutes later, the final trace of smugness had been wiped from Ty's face. His "leads" looked good to him, but once the group had dived into the details, they had vanished like the morning dew. Every single "lead" was unqualified. Not one had a definite target closing date, and the "next step" for all them followed the same theme.

"I'm playing golf with him next week."

"I had lunch with him yesterday, and I think it'll be a go."

"I think I can score T-Wolves tickets for them—they love their hoops at that place!"

It's all about entertainment, Joe thought wonderingly. Finally he put a stop to it. "Ty, let's pin this down. Dayton Industries—Are they actually looking for a new firm?"

"Well, no," Ty admitted, "but I think that could change."

"Braxton Enterprises—how about them?"

"I'm working on it," he said in a pained voice.

Joe squinted at the list again. "Here's another big one . . . ninety thousand dollars, Thousand Lake Realty. Status on them?"

"They're thinking about making a move."

Joe tried to keep the exasperation out of his voice. "Ty. I know the CEO at Thousand Lake. They've been with the same CPA firm for as long as I can remember. Do you have a reason—not hope, but a *reason*—for thinking they might move?"

"Yeah, I met with their new marketing guy—we had dinner last week at the club—and he's gonna get me introduced around to the execs."

"Ty, that's not a lead, that's a wing and a prayer!"

Feeling doomed, Joe nonetheless decided to try one more. "Wolfe-Stout Industries?"

"Working on it, Joe. And I think it might come through . . . any day now." Ty's voice had taken on a petulant, defensive tone, and partners were beginning to shift in their chairs. Joe realized it was time to shut down this line of inquiry, but Tiff, in her innocence, did not.

"All right," she piped up, "when you add all these new leads of Ty's onto what we had before, that brings us to . . . Now wait a second, I think I may have misadded . . . I want to double-check this . . . " Tiff's voice trailed off, and now half the partners were gazing at the ceiling or shaking their heads. *This must be what the ninth ring of hell feels like,* Joe thought.

"Tiff, no need," he said miserably. "Just leave it the way it was."

He leaned back into the numbers. "That'll bring us," he summarized, "to about one-point-one million in the pipeline." As he looked around the table, he saw satisfied nods and smiles. "Fifty-nine opportunities in all, with an average 'opportunity size' of just under nineteen thousand.

"Our firm generates around twenty-two million in revenue a year, so this represents about five percent of annual revenue." More smiles and nods, as partners looked at each other in congratulation. He decided to drop the bomb.

"Whoa, slow down a sec. That may sound great to you, but there's something you don't know. The highest-growth firms of our size have *twenty* percent, not five, in their pipeline at all times." He gave the news a moment to sink in. "That means that to be high growth, we need to have roughly four times the leads we have now." He paused again, then added the clincher. "Even modest-growth firms have ten percent in their pipelines.

"We've got our work cut out for us," he finished frankly. "What's more, I'm sure many of you noticed that the lion's share of the leads came from just a few niches, from a handful of partners. That needs to change too."

"So what you're telling us"—Frank put in, leaning forward, elbows on the table—"what we know now that we didn't two hours ago, is that this firm is *not* doing all that well. So how is that supposed to help?

Doesn't this just undermine our efforts, our enthusiasm? Isn't doom and gloom counterproductive?"

Judging from the astonished looks on many faces around the table, Joe knew he wasn't the only one marveling at the enormous irony of Frank Pierce—naysayer supreme—complaining that the meeting's tone was too negative. "No, Frank," Joe said firmly. "The first step to getting where we need to be is understanding where we are now, both strengths and weaknesses. In this case, ignorance is definitely *not* bliss."

To cut off any further discussion along this track, Joe concluded, "Anyway, here's what I want you all to do. Go back and think about this—your business opportunities—some more. Think about every last prospect you know of: anything that's been hanging out in the back of your mind, that note that you stuck in your drawer last month, everything. Then we'll get together again soon and put together a true, complete inventory. That'll give us a better take on where we stand."

Joe picked up his papers, stood, and strode from the room alone. When he reached his office, he closed the door and collapsed into his desk chair. After a moment, he leaned back and began massaging his temples, then reached into his desk drawer to grab some aspirin. He had a headache, but what's more, he was depressed.

Tiff's Big Surprise

Joe rubbed his temples and tried to think—tried, that is, to think of something positive to think about.

Why not be honest about it? he thought. Things were clearly worse than he'd realized. His partner group consisted of a bunch of Lone Rangers who showed little interest in working together. It was clear that there was no effective leadership structure, and the people who spoke loudest generally had the least to say. *It's as if we've been asleep at the switch—and that includes me—for years now, and this whole firm has been coasting on past glories.*

Joe was keenly aware that the infrastructure in place did not support growth. He winced as snippets from the just-concluded meeting flashed through his mind: Tiff bungling the addition on a spreadsheet, then fumbling for a calculator and trying in vain to carry out simple addition in her head. Ty, with his head full of jargon ("That's a suspect!"), yet completely unable to see that every single "lead" on the laundry list he called a pipeline was a suspect. Tiff, the marketing director they laughed at. Ty, the business developer no partner took seriously. Were they wrong? Joe asked himself. Based on what he'd just seen, he had to concede that there was merit in the disdain.

He sighed. He remembered a comment Alex had made about the importance of having highly qualified business development and marketing people on staff. "Can you imagine one of our clients having no vice president of sales? There'd be nothing but a bunch of sales people running around."

His reverie was broken by a knock. He looked up to see Tiff stepping into his office.

"I just wanted to check in with you and tell you how fantastic I thought our first pipeline meeting was. Wow! There's so much more to this, and it's so exciting!" she enthused.

Tiff was carrying a small parcel, and she started to open it, then stopped. "When I got back to my office, this was waiting for me, and the timing is just so perfect!" she chirped. "I just could not wait to come and show you. In every conceivable way, Crandall & Potter is ready to move ahead. Look what I've got!"

Tiff opened the box with a flourish and proudly produced . . . a water bottle. A deep-blue plastic water bottle embossed in white.

"Isn't this sooooo cool?" she asked, holding the bottle up and turning it this way and that, as if to admire it by catching imaginary rays of sunlight on an imaginary glass surface. "It's Crandall & Potter's new logo! On this sleek new bottle, with a new ergonomic design for sure, easy handling, even with sweaty hands! *And—just—in—time* for the unveiling of the new C&P!"

Joe reached inside to try to muster some thread of enthusiasm, but it simply wouldn't come. So he leaned forward, frowning, and said, "That's fine, Tiff, fine. But . . . " Tiff's face fell, and Joe felt the familiar tug of guilt, as if he were this young woman's father, for heaven's sake, and it was his job to cheer her every effort.

"The thing is, Tiff, the changes we're making here are going to go much, much deeper than a new logo or another freebie for the clients. And, since you're here right now, this gives us a great chance to talk. I'd like to start by going over the changes I see coming in your role."

Tiff dropped to the edge of a chair, wariness writ large on her face.

Joe caught himself trying to be reassuring. "It's nothing bad; nothing's wrong. In fact, just the opposite. With the changes I have in mind for this firm, your role is going to become much greater. I want you to be a key player in the future—hey, you may not even recognize your job six months from now!

"Tiff, when I was in Philadelphia, I met this amazing woman—actually, she was just part of an amazing group of partners and top staff at a CPA firm that used to be a lot like us, and now they're setting the world on fire. They do things very differently there, Tiff, and we're going to model our growth after theirs.

"This morning's meeting was just the beginning. I haven't even begun to outline all the changes I have in mind for you . . . Tiff?"

Joe's focus had shifted from Tiff's face as he spoke, and when he looked back, he could see that her faced had blanched. "Tiff."

"I'm okay, Joe. It's just—this is a lot to take in at one time. I thought . . . I thought my job was to provide marketing support." Her voice sounded plaintive. "That's what I was hired for, *trained* for. So I guess I'm wondering . . . what else did you have in mind for me, exactly?"

Joe's spirit plummeted. It seemed increasingly clear that Ty had been a bad hire; was he now stuck with a second one as well? Maybe not, he told himself; Tiff had performed well enough in the job that existed earlier. Was she capable of thinking strategically, though? That's what they needed from her—what they had to have—in order to get to the next level.

Ergonomic water bottles! Yikes!

There was another knock at the door, and Joe looked over quickly, thankful for a graceful ticket out of this conversation.

Jackie was standing in the doorway with a sheaf of papers in her hand. "I've got those segment numbers for you, Joe. I can come back, but you said you wanted them ASAP."

"No, that's right; come on in. We were just finishing up here."

He turned his attention back to Tiff. "Let's let this go for now, and we'll come back to it later, okay? Just give what I said some thought."

Tiff nodded uncertainly, picked up her package, and slipped quietly past Jackie and down the hall.

Time for a Change

Joe gazed at the document Jackie had handed him. It was not good news. The revenue stream was just as out of balance as the leads were.

Revenue from audits made up fully 30 percent of the revenue stream. And in charge of audit was . . . Joe groaned. The firm was well covered in terms of delivery of audit services. Where strategy was concerned, though, the sad truth was that *nobody* was in charge of audit, nobody was responsible for crafting strategic direction in the segment or looking out for its financial health. Nobody was in charge of a segment that represented a full third of their revenue!

Joe shuddered, all too easily imagining Alex's reaction. He could hear the conversation in his head:

Alex: Who has strategic ownership of that segment?
Joe: Well, no one person specifically; we treat it as an "at large" responsibility.
Alex: So how are strategies for the segment developed?
Joe: The partners get together and look at the numbers, then decide where we need to go from there.
Alex: How effective is that in terms of generating an actual strategy, then implementing it?
Joe shook his head glumly. He knew how it was done at Alex's firm, because he'd been there and seen it. Alex's segment leaders actually

owned revenue and profit responsibilities, and they were accountable for the direction of their segments. Everyone who carried out the work might not report to those leaders, but they still managed to achieve a very strong staff function, and there was no uncertainty about the chain of command.

At C&P, of course, Charles had by far the largest chunk of audit revenue. If Joe named Charles, the natural choice, as audit segment leader, Charles would assume responsibility for 30 percent of the firm's revenue. *Ye gods, what a scary thought!*

Still, might even Charles be better than having no one own it? Joe thought back to Charles's performance at the pipeline meeting, and he honestly wasn't sure.

Then he acknowledged the other part of the problem: Charles had no desire to be responsible for strategic direction; with him, it was all delivery, no strategy or growth. That failing, of course, was clearly reflected in the firm's current plight. How many top 100 firms, Joe wondered, completely missed the boat on 404 work? Or on SAS 70, another outgrowth of auditing changes?

He remembered something he'd heard Alex repeat more than once. "Delivery is *today's* work; strategy is *tomorrow's*." So simple, and yet light-years beyond where they were.

How did Charles respond when you challenged him to step up to the plate? Joe thought again ruefully of that conversation about 404 work. "It's not what we do, Joe," Charles had said, managing to convey a hint of pity that Joe had not managed to figure that out on his own. "Trust me, we don't need to go there."

Charles had been wrong, of course, and his head-in-the-sand approach—his resistance to change, really—had cost the firm dearly. At the Chicago meeting, Joe had heard one person after another describe the gigantic growth their firms had achieved through work in 404s and the related efforts—SAS 70, fraud and forensics, internal audits—that had followed.

How does Charles always get his way? Joe wondered. He knew that where ongoing work was concerned, people acceded to Charles because of his formidable technical expertise. But Joe also knew that quality assurance had gotten out of hand, and realization was down.

These were not, unfortunately, issues that held any interest for Charles. Moreover, whenever such matters were broached, Charles would summon up the spectre of Enron and Arthur Andersen, driving the fear of God deep into every single partner.

Joe spent a moment thinking about that. He knew operating from fear was never the right way to go, yet Charles wielded fear like a weapon to stave off all challenges.

Had Joe been just as much a slave to fear on his own, for his own unfathomable reasons? If so, it was time for a change in more ways than one.

Bombs Away!

Joe looked up to see Charles sidling into his office. Terrific! he thought. This may be just the right time to broach the subject—after all, he came to me!

It was late Monday morning, five days after the tumultuous partners' meeting, and Joe had spent every one of those days deep in thought. One key to his firm's future direction lay in choosing the right people for strategic responsibility. And the audit segment was key, making up, as it did, about a third of the firm's business. Was Charles up to taking on strategic ownership of the audit segment? Could he be made to understand what an honor it was? Would he agree to do so? Finally, if he did, could he carry it out enthusiastically?

A positive answer, Joe knew, could mean a huge leap forward, but his practical nature made him acknowledge that the path was littered with perils. First, Charles might not appreciate the nature of the responsibility. Being involved in every detail of audit delivery was a far cry from developing the segment, a task that required a different set of skills. (Joe even questioned whether Charles wanted to possess skills other than those that made him guru of audit.)

Second, even if Charles took on the new duties, there were no guarantees about how he would handle them. Even if I can persuade him that it makes sense to step up to a greater leadership role and be more of a team player, Joe wondered, does he even know how? Is that something you can teach?

Well, he decided, nothing ventured, nothing gained. He leaned forward to survey the audit guru, who sat casually, one leg draped over the other, an elbow propped on one arm of the chair. Charles was speaking. "Joe, I'm afraid I must come to you once more on behalf of my auditors, who are again being ridden roughshod over. I understand the firm is looking at moving the break room to the other side of the floor, and I want to discuss it with you.

"My auditors are upset, Joe, and I believe they have a legitimate grievance. This move seems to be favoring the tax department yet again." Joe sagged against the back of his chair, mouth slack with disbelief, but Charles took no notice. "Last year the tax department was the first area chosen for remodeling. Then they got an extra bathroom on their side. Now this. Are you trying to run off all the auditors?"

Joe was momentarily at a loss for words. Talk about sweating the small stuff! he thought. I need this guy to apply himself to the growth of the audit department, and he's tracking break rooms and bathrooms! Holy Morticia!

Joe took a moment to collect himself. "That's a valid point, Charles, and I'll keep it in mind. Certainly, no, there was no intention to slight the auditors in any way. While you're here, though," he continued, "I want to follow up with you on a different subject. You know that I've determined to try to take this firm in a new direction. That's why we had our first pipeline meeting last week, and that's what, well, what everything here at Crandall & Potter is pointed toward these days.

"But I've got one big gap." Joe gazed intently at Charles, hoping to see his intensity returned, but Charles seemed just as nonchalant as when he'd dropped carelessly into the chair.

"You know how hugely important the audit segment is to this firm," Joe plowed ahead. "And because it's so important, heck, crucial, to us, choosing the right person to head it up is key."

At last Charles was beginning to look mildly intrigued. "I'm in charge of audit, Joe," he said placidly.

"Audit delivery, yes, Charles, certainly, but I'm speaking in terms of growth. I need to name someone as segment leader in audit, and that person will have real ownership . . . of everything, from driving revenues and profits to determining"—Joe remembered just in time that he'd decided to avoid using the word "strategic" with Charles—"um, overall direction for the segment. You know how it is . . . this firm is getting too large for me to think about the strategic direction"—*Blast it!*—"and financial health of all the service lines and industries. I need to share that responsibility with you partners, and *you* have to tell *me* where we should be headed, not the reverse."

Joe plunged forward with his presentation, though Charles's deadpan expression had alarm bells ringing loudly in his head. "Who else knows that segment the way you do, Charles? Who else has the command? Not only the technical command, but the knowledge of who we are and what we are, from our services to staffing, plus the whole range of clients, top to bottom.

"Just look at the client you pulled in last week, Swanson Products. That's a huge feather in our cap, not to mention the enormous revenue enhancement it brings, and there's no one else who could have handled it, brought it off, the way you did." Joe could tell that he was slipping badly, anxious as he was to secure Charles's agreement—to something, anything. He knew he was speeding up nervously as he went along, but he also felt like he was speaking into a void. He knew he shouldn't press, that the lack of response was a clear message in itself, but somehow he couldn't let go of his need to press on and, well, get someplace with this.

Charles started to shake his head slowly, but Joe plowed ahead anyway. "All right, I know, Kevin will be part of that, since it's audit and tax work. But, still, you're key here, and I want you to think about taking the lead—"

Joe stopped as he noticed the frankly impatient look that had come over Charles's face.

"You know, Joe, if it's really important to you to talk to me about that, I will, but you know my fundamental view on such matters. I'm a technician, one of the very best in my field. I am not a rainmaker; that's not what I went to college to become. Why should my time be wasted on such trivialities as strategic planning and growth?" Charles shrugged. "I'm not a rainmaker, and I don't intend to become one."

Joe's mind was in a whirl. Is it possible, he asked himself, that this guy doesn't realize what he's done? He's just finished blowing off, in one short sentence, an assignment his firm's managing partner labeled key!

Joe sat back in his chair. "You want to take a pass, huh?"

"Oh, absolutely," Charles replied serenely. "You know, maybe this is something we should go out of house for. Maybe hire some young blood, somebody who's trying to break into the business. That might work, yes," Charles said, his sight trained on a spot above and slightly to the left of Joe's head. "Let them spend their time playing with spreadsheets keeping track of projects."

"Charles, I hardly think you understand," Joe protested. "This position, audit segment leader—this person will head up the entire audit operation."

"Not me," Charles replied complacently. "They won't head up me. I'll just carry on with my work as usual. And they certainly won't have any say in quality control or audit methodologies."

Joe sat for a moment, nonplussed. Then he was struck by the realization that this was, in effect, his answer. He had tried to nominate Charles for this responsibility, and Charles had passed. So the solution would have to come from another direction, and it would.

"All right, Charles," he said. "I appreciate your being so frank with me."

"Not at all," Charles said, standing and starting for the door. Then he stopped abruptly and slapped his forehead. "Oh, one other thing . . . " He dropped back into his chair and heaved a small sigh. "Referencing what you mentioned just before. I'm afraid I have some rather disappointing news in that regard." Joe sat back in his chair, his mind already racing forward with the problem of finding an audit segment leader and expecting to hear, well, perhaps that Charles's secretary needed some unscheduled time off to attend to family matters, or that the soda machine in the lunchroom was leaking again.

"It looks as if we didn't get Swanson after all."

There was complete stillness for a few moments, as if the very air had been suctioned out of the room. Then Joe cocked his head slightly to the right, certain he could not possibly have understood right. "Say that again?"

"We didn't get the client we discussed. Swanson Products. Audit and tax engagement. It didn't work out."

Joe still didn't move, and Charles stood to go. "So I suppose we'll need to take it off your pipeline list. Shall I e-mail Tiffany about that?"

Not in the Bag after All

Joe could feel his face flushing, and he fought for words and the control to deliver them. "What happened?" he finally managed.

"Well, I heard from Taylor DiStefano earlier this morning, and our price was too high."

Joe sought to maintain a level tone of voice. "Charles, last week you said, both in the partners' meeting and privately with me later that afternoon, that that opportunity was well in hand." Joe had no need to consult his notes; the details were seared into his brain. "You said, when we talked, that you expected it to close within two weeks at the outside. There was *no* sense of urgency on your part, Charles, no sense that any additional attention was needed. My goodness, you practically shoved Kevin and Ty out of your way. Not only did you fail to consult them at any point, but you *insisted* at the meeting that involvement from Kevin would be superfluous.

"Remember that meeting, Charles? You said all that was lacking was formal approval by the Swanson board, and that they'd be meeting by week's end to confirm it. You said it was on—your words—'the very verge of being closed.' When I checked back with you last Friday afternoon, you said you'd talked with Taylor again, and everything was still on target. Dash it, Charles, *you said it was in the* bag!"

"Well, clearly, Joe, I was mistaken. Really"—and here Charles took the opportunity to straighten in his chair and square his shoulders—"I don't quite understand why you seem so, well, to be frank, so almost hostile about it. It was a job. We thought we had it. We didn't. We'll get another. Life goes on."

Joe sat back in his chair, unbelieving. He would not have thought, were he not seeing it himself, that one of his most senior partners could be so blasé about losing such a huge opportunity.

He gathered himself and spoke with difficulty. "All right, that's all, Charles. Oh, one more thing. When did you find out?"

"Taylor called me a little while ago . . . but I also ran into him on the course Saturday morning, and he sidestepped my suggestion of lunch after we'd finished our rounds. I must say that did give me brief pause."

"Did you consider phoning Ty at that point? Or calling Kevin in? Or doing *anything* to see if we could save this, if you thought it was going down?"

Charles gazed at Joe, incredulous. "You're actually suggesting that Kevin—or, worse, that lummox Tyler—could have succeeded where I did not? Honestly, Joe, I wonder about you sometimes."

And with those words of wisdom, Charles betook himself out of Joe's office and set off for his own.

The news spread like wildfire. Up and down the halls, over desks and lunch tables, everyone from filing clerks to partners was buzzing over the news.

Charles had let the cat out of the bag while Joe was still sitting in his office considering options. Charles had mentioned it to his secretary and dashed off an e-mail message to Tiff, and just like that, the word was out.

Reaction was swift, and sharp. By two o'clock, many of the senior partners were huddled in a corridor near Kevin's office. He'd been barricaded behind his desk, working on a tax opinion, and had run into Frank Pierce when he stepped away to carry out a personal errand. Frank had delivered the bombshell, and the group of partners had mushroomed. Now there were eight in all, including Kevin, Frank, Harold Brumlow, Ben Spencer, Durwood Poole, Smith Smoot, and Matthew Hanover. Eric had been the last to join the group, arriving a few minutes ago.

"This is preposterous!" Harold was saying. "Why, he said it was all sewn up! He said it was in the bag!"

"What he actually said," Eric pointed out, "if I remember correctly, is that it was well in hand, and that he felt quite confident about it."

"Well, then, he was wrong, wasn't he?" Harold sneered.

"The problem isn't so much what he said or didn't say," Kevin declared, "it's how he went about the whole thing. He didn't consult me, and a big piece of the work is tax, which is my area."

"That's true, Kevin," Durwood Poole put in. "But it's also hardly surprising. Charles never talks to anybody. Why would he start now?"

"That's a good point," Matthew said. "We maybe should be looking at this as a communications problem. So then the question becomes, How can we communicate more effectively with each other? Can we put a better system in place for that?"

"That's nonsense!" Frank snapped.

"I have to agree," Ben said. "Doesn't matter if you're using BlackBerries or tin cans with string, Charles isn't going to bother. He goes his own way. Always has."

"I think so too," Kevin said. "Just look what started this. An enormous opportunity, really just outstripping everything else on the horizon, and he kept it hidden in the audit department."

"Then maybe the problem is really management," Harold mused. "Don't we pay our managing partner to *manage the partners*? Isn't it his job to make things go smoothly?"

"I'm not sure that's fair," Eric put in. "Joe followed up on this as soon as he found out about it, last Wednesday. What was he supposed to do, *order* Charles to cooperate with Kevin and Ty?"

"Ty!" Harold snorted. "Give me a break! What earthly difference would that clown have made? With his *pinkie ring*!" he spat.

Eric opened his mouth to speak, but stopped as he spotted Charles heading toward the group. "Hello, Charles," he said with a shake of his head. "We heard about Swanson. Tough luck."

Charles waved an arm in dismissal. "There'll be others." He started to step on past the group, but Durwood placed a hand on his arm.

"Charles, we're trying to put some perspective on this thing. This was a huge opportunity for the firm. I think I probably speak for all of us when I say we'd come to count on that business, based on your assurances last Wednesday. It might help if you could provide some insight into what went wrong."

Charles tilted his head to the side as he regarded his fellow partners. "Well," he said judiciously, "I don't have a great many details. Taylor DiStefano gave me to understand that they simply decided to stay with Diggs & Carey, not to make a move after all."

"But why? Why did they so decide?"

"He said our price was too high, and Diggs & Carey dropped their price dramatically."

"But I thought they weren't happy with Diggs & Carey. That's what you said," Frank pressed. "Didn't you say that?"

"Yes. That's true." Charles looked and sounded exasperated. "Look. Taylor told me they'd had some issues with Diggs & Carey in the past, and they didn't think they could be resolved, and then it turned out they could be. And were. So that's all there is to it. There was nothing we could do."

"But we were so close," Kevin growled. "And we could have adjusted our price too. Did you have any idea it was falling apart?"

"Not really," Charles said. "I did run into Taylor Saturday morning at the club, and I suggested lunch, and he demurred. Really, I thought that was quite a gesture on my part. You know how much I detest business lunches. So I truly did go quite the extra mile."

"If you had an idea on Saturday, you could have called me," Kevin insisted. "Maybe we could have done something together to head this off. At least we might have found out it was a price issue and had a chance to respond."

"There's also Ty," Eric pointed out. "Why didn't you give Ty a call? The gladhanding thing—that's supposed to be his bailiwick."

Charles looked at Eric as if he'd grown horns. "Surely you're not serious. Call in Blond Boy to help on one of *my clients*?"

"They weren't your clients yet," Eric reminded him. "They were prospects, and that's Ty's specialty."

Charles could feel a consensus building against him. He should have called Kevin, he should have called Ty—what difference did it make? He hadn't called anybody, and so what? That was simply the way he did things. Didn't they all know that?

Still, it looked as if bold action was in order here. Charles decided quickly. "What difference would it have made?" he demanded harshly. "You all know Ty. You know how little he brings to the table. Look at the situation! A very large, privately held company, very sedate, very old school, with highly complex tax and audit issues—and they thought they wanted to make a change. Thought they wanted to bring in somebody new. Can any one of you imagine Ty being helpful in that situation?"

Sensing he'd struck gold, Charles took the opportunity to move his eyes around the circle, taking in each partner in turn. "No, I thought not," he concluded. "Ty may be good at gaining admission to popular sporting events, but as a serious colleague in this field, he's a joke." With that, Charles strode off.

After a moment, murmuring set in among the partners. But all fell silent when Ty turned a corner and came ambling into view. "Hey, guys. What's going on?" He stopped and then gave a little shrug and a laugh. "Hey, where's the funeral?"

Looking for a Fall Guy

At last Eric broke the silence. "Um, you haven't heard?"

"Heard what?" Ty asked.

"Swanson fell through," Eric said succinctly.

"You're kidding, right?"

"We don't kid about things like that, Ty," Kevin said ominously.

"Wow," Ty breathed. "I'll bet Joe is having one sweet conniption right now."

Silence descended again as the partners stood uncomfortably, studying their shoes. "How'd it happen?" Ty finally asked.

When no one answered immediately, Eric again stepped into the gap. "Apparently they decided not to leave their old firm. We were told our price was too high."

Ty chuckled as he leaned one shoulder against the wall. "That's always the reason they give—but there's almost always more to it than that. Well, Joe better drag out that old pipeline, don't you think, guys?" Ty kidded. "And get out the old red ink pen?" No one laughed, and Ty straightened up. "Do you think I should go talk to him?"

"It's a little late for talking now," Smith pointed out. "The business is lost. The time for talking was last week, when Charles was trying to pin down the engagement. That's when you should have been able to talk. To make a difference. To help Charles win this one."

"Hey, buddy, I totally agree. Totally," Ty chirped. "Tell you what I'll do. I'll go talk to him now."

"To Charles?" Kevin asked. He couldn't believe he'd heard properly.

"Sure. Now's the best time in the world for it. Make him see his mistake. Point out that if he'd brought Ty in, which he should have as we all know, it might have turned out differently. Ty could've helped save his bacon. See you guys." And with a jaunty salute, Ty sauntered off down the hall, this time, purportedly, in search of Charles. But then they saw him stick his head into the business center office and duck through the door. Since he was carrying no papers to copy or transmit, the likelihood seemed high that it was a social detour.

"Our business developer," Harold said savagely. "He understands nothing! Brings nothing! He is nothing!"

Eric saw the looks that were going round the circle and the nods being exchanged.

"And look how much we're paying him!" Harold added.

"That's a point," Frank allowed.

"What a mess," Kevin said with disgust. "Joe and his bright ideas. He's the one who hired Ty. He's the one who came up with this grand new scheme. It sounded pretty terrific last Wednesday. What does it feel like now, boys?"

They looked at each other, and more nods were exchanged.

"Yep, that's about it," Kevin said.

Finding Joe's door closed, Kevin knocked sharply and then opened the door and entered without waiting for an invitation. Eric followed. Eric lowered himself into a chair, but Kevin strode to the edge of Joe's desk and rapped a knuckle on the desktop.

"This issue with Swanson Products," he began balefully. "This is a disaster for Crandall & Potter, Joe, and it absolutely needn't have been."

Joe nodded. "I agree totally, Kevin. Why don't you have a seat and we'll talk about it."

"We'll talk, standing or sitting," Kevin groused, but he dropped into a chair nonetheless. "I don't know who to be angriest with—Charles, for hiding this enormous opportunity under his coattail until it was too late. Ty, for being worthless on something like this. Or you, for running the ship that just struck the iceberg."

Joe took a deep breath and let it out slowly. "All right, I understand your frustration with Charles. I feel the same way; he mishandled this completely. Of course it's vintage Charles all the way, but that hardly makes it easier to swallow. And you can blame me if you want. But what's Ty got to do with it? He was left out in the cold as much as you were."

"The point," Kevin said angrily, "is that I *could* have helped, had I been given the chance. Ty *couldn't*."

"Explain," Joe said curtly.

"I assume you mean explain about Ty. All right. We were just standing in the hall talking with Charles about what happened, and he made a point I consider apposite. Granted, Ty was left out of the loop—but would it have made any difference if he'd been in?

"Think about this company, Joe. Swanson Products. They're as conservative as they come, they're midwestern business royalty. They behave, in everything, including negotiations, like complete gentlemen. *They don't wear pinkie rings!*"

"Now hold it a second," Joe said testily. "Ty makes an effort to match his personal attire to the client at hand."

Kevin waved away the objection and continued. "Their tax issues are complex, and they don't negotiate at basketball games. In fact, they are the polar opposite of everything Ty is—they're not flashy, they're not surface, they're not glib. Honestly, Joe, you've met these guys. If you were Charles, would you have wanted to go into a meeting with them with Ty at your side? I'll be honest, I don't blame him for leaving Ty out."

"He left you out too," Joe said pointedly.

"Yeah, and that's wrong. But I think it's about time to face facts. Your Boy Wonder business developer is a disaster!"

"Can we try to keep this a little less personal?" Eric put in. "Focus on the issues?"

"This is the issue!" Kevin snapped. "Business developer is a big job, and we have a nincompoop filling it!"

"And the partners are nincompoops too?" Joe responded. "It wasn't Ty who hid this in his skirts, Kevin. Partners are supposed to know better."

"You're right, Joe, Charles made a mistake. But he's Charles, for heaven's sake, and it's exactly the kind of mistake we all know he's going to make—will *continue* to make. My goodness, if Charles sits in that partner's chair for fifty more years, he'll handle opportunities the exact same way for fifty more years. He'll never change.

"Ty's a different matter. He's an employee—one with a high-sounding title, but an employee just the same. And I maintain, and I think most of the partners will be with me on this, that Ty is not suited to the position he holds in this firm. Respectfully, Joe, I suggest that it's time to make a change."

Hoping to furnish Joe with additional information before he committed himself, Eric spoke quickly. "Joe, I have to say that I think the trend is moving in that direction—"

But Joe cut him off. "No one's being fired right now. We're at the beginning of a long process of evaluation and change. We are not jumping the gun by making a scapegoat of Ty."

Kevin's face twisted. "Especially not since Ty happens to be your guy, right, Joe? You hired him, your credibility's on the line, and you couldn't possibly have messed up. Right. Well, we'll see. We'll see how things play out.

"But I've got a tip for you, Joe. You're the one who set up that meeting last week to go over new prospects. You're the one who flushed out this Swanson thing and made it the centerpiece for growth. You're the one who told us how much new business we need to have in our 'pipeline,' and you're the one who said that, even with Swanson under our belts, we were still coming up short.

"And now we've lost Swanson! So somebody's going to take the fall for this, they've got to. And here's the news flash: The partners will line up behind a fellow partner. As far as Ty is concerned, consensus is building that he's a joke. So we'll see who has the last laugh."

Kevin stood without another word, turned on his heel, and departed.

Joe looked at Eric, who was shifting uncomfortably in his seat. "Well, maybe he's right, and maybe he's not," Joe said. "I can't believe Charles will be able to deflect all the criticism about Swanson onto Ty."

"He already took a pretty fair crack at it," Eric said, taking a few moments to fill Joe in on the impromptu meeting in the hall. "It makes sense—in practical terms anyway. Who wants to be mad at Charles? Who can afford to be? Whereas Ty is a natural target. And honestly, Joe, he doesn't help his case much."

"You too, huh?" Joe snapped.

"Come on, Joe, be fair. I told you what happened in the hall. He just doesn't seem to get it. He almost thought it was funny. Or maybe he felt vindicated; I don't know. But the way to respond to a huge opportunity going up in smoke . . . making jokes about the MP taking a red pen to the pipeline? It's like he doesn't get the enormity of the situation.

"You saw Kevin back off at the meeting last Wednesday. He was really annoyed that he'd been left out, but his response was, Okay, so long as the opportunity's in hand, I'll step back. The business came first and his ego second. If you could've heard Ty today, you would have seen that he had it absolutely backward. It was okay that the business was lost, because he had his yuks. Ho ho, they should have called in Ty; he could've helped save the bacon! I don't think you would have liked it very much, Joe."

Eric took a deep breath and finished his thought. "But even more than that, when Charles was talking, when he was saying that Ty would've brought nothing to the table, there was this moment when the partners all looked at each other, and you could just see it clicking with every single one of them. Charles made some crack to the effect that Ty can get tickets to ball games, but he's useless in serious, complex opportunities. I think those partners agree, and I'd bet the others will too.

"I think you need to face facts, Joe," Eric said simply. "I think Ty is a liability."

"Great," Joe said glumly. "Before I had one liability—Charles and his stubbornness and narrow-mindedness. Now I have two."

"I'm Licked"

Joe walked to the window and gazed out for several minutes, trying to fight the feelings of hopelessness that were coursing through his body.

I thought I could do this! he told himself. *I thought I had the tools and the leadership skills!*

And maybe I do. But maybe it's just too far along in the process. If only I'd gotten started last June . . .

Joe shook himself out of his reverie. Speculation was idle and completely useless at this point. The issue was, what to do next? He started ticking off the major issues—Ty's perceived deficiencies, Charles's obtuseness, the lost opportunity at Swanson, the firm's understocked pipeline, the mutiny Eric had hinted was brewing among the partners . . . and oh, yes, Joe added, let's not forget our marketing director and her confounded water bottles. He slumped in his chair and found his eyes drawn to the phone. *I can pick it up right this minute and get help,* Joe thought. *Alex promised as much when we talked that last evening in Philadelphia.*

Joe hated to ask for help; it felt so much like failure. He recalled the look of skepticism on Alex's face and the words that had accompanied it. "You still think you can take it on single-handedly. You think you can slay this beast," Alex had said.

You were right, Alex, Joe thought as he reached to pick up the phone. *You could see it right then. I'm licked, and I need your help.*

"It takes a fair amount of confidence to be able to own up to your limitations," Alex said. "We'd all like to think we have all the answers."

"Seems I have hardly any," Joe replied honestly.

"I don't know about that," Alex chuckled. "You've decided to bring me in, and I'd have to say that's the right call."

"How do we get started?"

"Didn't you say your annual off-site meeting is coming up soon?"

"Right, it starts two weeks from this Thursday."

"Where exactly do you hold it; how far from Minneapolis? I assume all the major players will be there, right? What kind of agenda have you put together so far?"

"Whoa, slow down," Joe laughed. "Let's see. We always go to this little resort in Stillwater. It's about—oh, no more than an hour outside Minneapolis. We're pretty lucky that way; there aren't many places up here where you can play golf in late October!

"Agenda—well, the meetings generally follow the same format. Part of the time—most of it, really—is spent relaxing together, you know, to renew the bonds that can fray over the course of a year. This year, I think that may be especially important, in light of recent developments. There seems to be a rift growing between some of the partners and the key staff, in particular our business developer.

"Let's see," Joe went on. "We spend some time focusing in on strategic planning—you know, where we've been, where everybody expects the next year to take us. We flesh out differences in outlook among the partners, play some more golf . . . you know how it goes, Alex. These things run pretty much to form, don't they?"

"In all honesty, I have to say, Joe, that this one probably won't—run to form, that is. But here's a better way to put it: This year's meeting will establish a *new* form, set the stage for the new direction you're mapping out for Crandall & Potter."

"Fine," Joe replied. "Let's see, what didn't I address yet? Oh, yes, attendance at the retreat. All the partners will be there, of course, along with Jackie Brown, our COO."

"And your marketing and business development people, of course," Alex added.

"Well, no," Joe replied. "Just the partners and Jackie."

"Those two need to be there," Alex said firmly.

"The partners are not going to like that," Joe protested. "They like to think of this as their time alone—you know, like a little bit of a 'thank you' for their work all year long."

"Then they'll have to go without being thanked this year," Alex said dryly. "This is important to the firm, Joe. This is the annual strategy meeting, not a party." Joe was silent, and after a pause that stretched out to half a minute, Alex asked, "Who's managing this enterprise?" He then added, more lightheartedly, "Listen, Joe, there will be some tough calls ahead, guaranteed, but this is *not* one of them. This is one of the easy ones. *You* decide who comes." He then added, rather unpromisingly, Joe thought, "Trust me, by the time we're under way, gripes like this will be the least of your worries."

A few minutes later, it was all set. Alex had graciously agreed to come west to facilitate the retreat, and Joe had agreed to lay the groundwork according to Alex's detailed instructions. As Alex began to outline some of the preparations, Joe felt the first pangs of misgivings.

"There's gonna be real resistance, Alex," he said. "These partners are used to packing up their golf clubs and driving over to Stillwater for two and a half days of golf and fine dining, with a little idle chatter thrown in to salve their consciences about the write-off. They're going to resent the notion of having to do any real work."

"That's not all they're going to resent," Alex replied candidly. "Which leads me to this: I think it might be wise for you to take a couple of days to go over all this again before you make any final commitment. This course of action, once you embark on it, is irrevocable. You won't be able to turn back; you won't even be able to change course much to speak of.

"And it won't be easy; that I can guarantee."

Joe felt the need for some reassurance. "You've done this before with other firms."

"I have," Alex said, "more than once. And I'll be honest and tell you that it's likely to be difficult and strenuous. There'll be times during the weekend when you'll be extremely uncomfortable, and there'll be times when you may wish you'd never started."

"That's hardly encouraging," Joe said.

"Yes, but that's not the whole story. First there's the issue of how much choice you really have, and the answer is not much, if you want to turn your firm around. The impetus doesn't have to come from me, of course, but some skilled guidance is going to be needed for you to do that. The events of the past week bear that out, I'd say. You gave it your best shot on your own, and you learned you need help. There's no shame in that, Joe; we all need to call in experts from time to time.

"The rest of the story involves the likely outcome, both ways—with and without changes to your firm. Without changes, you know the score. Crandall & Potter is behind its competitors, and the gap keeps growing every day.

"With changes, though–that's the pot of gold at the end of the rainbow. That's what makes it all worth it—the agonizing over the need for change, the dodging all the darts that'll come your way, the making tough decisions and sticking to them.

"If you do all that, then you'll get the reward. You'll have Crandall & Potter on a solid foundation, with a forward-looking plan. And you'll have the right people in place to carry out the plan. I haven't forgotten what you told me Al Potter meant to you, the responsibility you feel to him. If you follow through all the way, Joe, at the end you may feel like you've walked through hell, but you'll also feel Al Potter smiling down on you from heaven. Hold onto that, because you'll need something to hold onto."

"Is that the way you felt about your father?" Joe asked.

"It is," Alex replied. "I knew his methods and way of doing business were nothing like mine, but the old gives way to the new. He wanted the firm he founded to prosper, and he wanted me to prosper with it. I'm sure Al Potter felt the same way about you."

Joe sat for a moment, amazed to find that he felt close to tears.

"We'll do it, Alex," he said at last. "I've thought about nothing else for days."

"Terrific," Alex said warmly. "We may have to grind some gears to do it, but together, we'll shift this business of yours into overdrive."

PART II

SHALL WE GROW?

Egos and Prejudices

The next week was a blur for Joe, full of preparations for the annual retreat. First on tap was a questionnaire, e-mailed to all partners and to every member of the staff, top to bottom, on Tuesday afternoon. The instructions stated that responses would be held in strict confidence, and that, in return, rigorous honesty was requested. Responses were to be directed to Jackie for compilation. The questionnaire was due back in one week's time.

Questions for more senior individuals included the following:

- What is the purpose of the annual retreat?
- Where should Crandall & Potter be headed in the next three years?
- How much growth would you like to see Crandall & Potter achieve?
- How much growth do you actually expect C&P to achieve?
- Has C&P achieved high enough growth over the past few years?

- Name the three greatest external threats that Crandall & Potter faces in the marketplace.
- Name the three greatest internal problems that Crandall & Potter faces.
- Name the top three opportunities for growth for Crandall & Potter.
- Do the partners and key staff at C&P function well together as a team?
- Do partners and staff more commonly pursue opportunities together, or separately, as individuals?
- On a scale of 1 to 10, how effective is our marketing director?
- On a scale of 1 to 10, how effective is our business developer?
- How effectively does the managing partner carry out his functions?
- What do you understand the role of the managing partner to be?

A different questionnaire went to every employee at Crandall & Potter, regardless of rank or responsibility. These questions—nearly 30 in all— were designed to probe for information about specific aspects of the firm's marketing, business development, and fulfillment practices, and client relations. On these questionnaires, the respondent was asked to evaluate, on a point scale, statements both broad ("Our efforts in business development are targeted toward the right kinds of clients") and narrow ("We meet deadlines without delays").

There were also a few open-ended questions, including, "If you could make one change to improve the effectiveness of our X department, what would it be?" That question was asked about two departments, marketing and business development.

Ty was overheard, in the lunchroom, sharing one of his responses with a secretary he'd run into there. "Nothing to it," he said with a laugh. "Just give Ty a raise and bump up his expense account. What I couldn't do . . . with a few more buckaroos!" Joe heard about that and cringed.

That Tuesday afternoon, as he assembled the "To" list on his e-mail invitation to the annual retreat, Joe struggled mightily within himself. He vividly recalled Alex's admonition that all key staffers must attend, but he had grave misgivings about the wisdom of bringing Tiff and Ty.

Where Tiff was concerned, part of Joe's struggle was an effort to divine his own motives. He couldn't shake the feeling that Tiff didn't belong at this meeting, but he knew that might be coming from his fear of being mortified by her behavior there.

What if she pulled another water bottle out of a box? Or, worse, a Crandall & Potter mousepad . . . or a golf towel . . . or coffee cup . . . Was this discomfort, this foreboding, an indication that Tiff was out of her league? Or was it simply a reflection of her obvious immaturity in her job, which might lead to embarrassment but nothing worse? If the first were true, there was no point in inviting her. If the second, Joe should simply buck up, swallow his pride, and bring her along, knowing they both might take some lumps if she blundered badly.

Ty seemed like an easier case, yet Joe's own inclinations were anti-thetical to the instructions Alex had given. With each passing day, Joe felt more strongly that it was time to admit that he'd chosen poorly when he hired Ty. It felt like time to take another look at the business developer position. But Alex had said all key staffers had to be at the retreat, and Ty was still part of that staff.

Oh, the heck with it, Joe thought. *I agreed to let Alex take the lead, so I might as well follow him. And forget about personalities; the marketing and business development people clearly belong at our main planning meeting.* So. He added both Tiff's and Ty's e-mail addresses to the partners' and Jackie Brown's, and hit Send.

It should be quite a gathering.

Reaction was almost instantaneous. Within three minutes, Joe had an e-mail reply from Kevin. "Staff doesn't come to ARs," he'd written. "Out of the question. Jackie can come as per usual, but not the two twerps."

Harold was more dramatic. Barely an hour after the message went out, he strode briskly into Joe's office, brandishing a printout of the message.

"This is completely unacceptable," he said firmly. "The annual retreat is for partners. It is our time together. This is nonsense." When Joe didn't respond, he went on. "You will please send out another message immediately rescinding this one and noting that attendance will be, as always, partners only."

"Jackie's not a partner, and she's been coming for years," Joe observed levelly.

"Yes, but in that case . . . " Harold stood for a moment, consulting his memory perhaps. "If she's come before, as you say, then yes, I suppose she can come again. But not those two! Who wants to play golf with that playboy?" he sneered. "Pinkie ring! Hah!" He turned abruptly and was gone.

Joe sighed and turned to his keyboard, bringing up a new message form, this time addressing it to partners only. "As you know, Crandall & Potter has engaged the services of a colleague who has facilitated retreats for numerous CPA firms, mostly on the East Coast," Joe wrote. "Because of his level of expertise, we have agreed to follow his lead as we go forward, both at this meeting and beyond. It was at his express suggestion that Tiff and Ty were invited to join us at this year's retreat. I would appreciate everyone's support in welcoming them with as much enthusiasm as you can muster."

Joe hit Send again and considered the matter settled.

The matter was not settled. By 11 o'clock the following morning, Joe had received e-mail messages from 13 of his 23 partners complaining about the "outrageous encroachment" (Frank Pierce's term) on a "traditional perk" (Durwood Poole's) reserved to partners. Frankly, Joe was surprised at the vehemence of the outburst. Even partners he thought of as reasonable exhibited pique at the suggestion that this traditional enclave, this perquisite of partnerly power, was being compromised. Just as Joe finished perusing Durwood's surly missive, Tiff stepped into his office, crimson faced and clearly uncomfortable.

"I want you to know how much I appreciate what you're trying to do for us," she began. "You want Ty and me to feel like we're really part of the team; you don't want us to feel left out. But some of these guys, these partners"—she took a moment to roll her eyes—"they just take it all so *seriously*. You'd think this was the Fountain of Youth, and somebody was trying to snatch their spot."

She held up her hands. "Joe, I just want you to know that my feelings won't be hurt if I don't go. And you can tell me what happened when you get back. It's okay; really, it is."

Joe sat for a moment, wondering whether to feel annoyed at Tiff's conception of the retreat as some sort of picnic from which she'd been excluded or to be grateful to her for trying to ease the discomfort of his position. Then a thought struck him.

"Talked to Ty?" he asked.

Tiff giggled. "Yeah, he's practically packed already. He thinks this shows he's moved up to the Big Time. He thinks he made a big splash at that pipeline meeting." Tiff's expression grew more serious. "You know how he is, Joe. He gets a little caught up sometimes."

Joe picked up a pencil and tapped the eraser lightly against the palm of his hand. "I'm not sure how it's going to come out, Tiff. I'll have to talk to a few of the partners. I'm not sure this is worth going to the mat for. In any case, I appreciate your coming in. What I said to you before still goes, by the way. You have a lot ahead of you here at this firm. We'll get 'em whipped into shape if it kills us!"

Thirty-five minutes later, Joe was putting the finishing touches on yet another e-mail message to his partners. "I've decided to accede to the deeply held belief of a number of partners that certain key staff should not be included in this year's annual retreat," he wrote. "But all partners should understand—if they do not already—that *change is coming* here at Crandall & Potter. This annual retreat will be unlike any you have ever attended, so come prepared for changes, even surprises.

"We have a very limited amount of time at this retreat, and a great deal of ground to cover. We will not waste time debating trivialities. I am asking you, for the good of the firm, to set aside your egos and prejudices and to come prepared to work, not relax.

"The purpose of this retreat is to see where we've been and decide where we're going. Every minute will count. We're talking about the future of our firm."

Setting the Stage

Joe's initial e-mail message to the partners had contained a broad outline for the retreat. Everyone would arrive by late Thursday afternoon, relax for a short period in their rooms, then meet for a casual dinner with no program.

Friday was packed full of activity, with sessions running from 8 to 5:30, with a brief time out for lunch. The executive committee—Kevin, Charles, and Eric, with Joe and Alex sitting in—would meet between 5:30 and dinner, at 7:30. Dinner would again be a casual affair.

Saturday would follow the same schedule through adjournment at 5:30 p.m.

Joe knew there'd be rumbles about the program, and he was certainly not disappointed. The partners really wanted golf and drinking, not heavy lifting, on the agenda. Frank was the most outspoken in voicing his resentment, but he was hardly alone. That entire week, Joe was unable to walk down the hall without hearing someone's voice raised in protest.

This is not the purpose annual retreats were intended to serve!

Partners work hard each year, and the retreat is one way the firm rewards them. How dare it be turned into a common workground?

When would there be time for golf? When would the partners find time to relax and socialize?

Indeed, who had ever even heard of such a thing? A working retreat? For years immemorial, stretching back to Al Potter himself, Crandall & Potter CPAs had made this annual sojourn to eat, drink, play golf, and renew the bonds of cordiality and camaraderie that held them fast during the rest of the year. How dare Joe try to change that now?

It was a tradition! Didn't he understand that?

At every protestation, Joe stopped, listened, and spoke briefly about the pressing need for change. At the beginning he made an honest effort to explain the reasoning behind the change. He gradually heard himself shift into defensiveness, and by Friday—three days after the message went out—he was rather clipped in his responses.

Everybody knew the score anyway. Joe was shooting the whole works, putting all his marbles, on this strategy. If it succeeded, terrific. If not, he was through as managing partner and, people gradually grew to believe, probably as any kind of partner at Crandall & Potter.

The executive committee had been tasked with responsibility for drumming up enthusiasm for the new approach, especially in advance of the retreat. In support of this effort, Joe had met briefly with them in his office on Thursday morning, to acquaint them with Alex's firm and detail the success he'd enjoyed in transforming it from a small, stagnant firm to one of the leading CPA firms on the East Coast. Joe outlined the plan for the upcoming retreat, including the fact that Alex would act as facilitator, a role he had played in similar situations before with notable success.

Eric threw himself into the effort with his usual enthusiasm, and Kevin, once he'd been placated on the matter of attendance at the retreat by lowly staff members, did his part as well. While Kevin never said so directly, privately he was pleased that Joe was finally taking action to kick the firm out of the doldrums. He kept that thought to himself, however.

Charles, not surprisingly, was a different matter altogether. Joe had been willing to overlook Charles's silence, but when he heard two secretaries giggling over a crack they'd heard Charles make ("I don't know what's worse—wasting time on golf and imbibing, or a bunch of 'strategic vision' nonsense!"), he confronted the wayward partner.

He got nowhere. Charles's stance was simple: He was due to rotate off the executive committee January first, which was fine with him, since he thought this new approach a load of hooey. It would be hypocritical or worse for him to voice an enthusiasm he did not feel—and he doubted that anyone would buy it anyway. So he would agree to keep his silence henceforth, but that was the most he felt he could in good conscience offer.

Joe swallowed his anger and said, "See that you do keep silent then, Charles. No more underhanded gibes." He walked away, feeling frustrated and stymied, but doubtful that anything would be gained by pushing the matter.

Alex couldn't possibly have had a partner as irritating as Charles! Joe was certain of it.

Ah, if only Alex had heard that thought, the one ringing in Joe's head. Alex could have assured Joe that *every* firm has its Charles.

There was one more aspect to the situation. Joe had made it plain that he expected the partners in particular, in completing their questionnaires, to provide "full, thoughtful responses." Jackie was instructed to tally the answers, and Joe had intended to instruct her to assess each partner's response for thoughtfulness and to send back any that fell short. Alex pointed out, though, that everything had to be anonymous.

If Joe had had his way, several responses would have gone back for a complete do-over. The biggest offenders? Harold and Charles, of course. Who else?

The Calm before the Storm

Joe and Alex had decided to stick to the tradition that the Thursday dinner be mainly social. Alex wanted the opportunity to study the partners' interactions, to size them up as individuals and as a group. The two had left it open as to whether Alex would make any kind of opening statement at tonight's dinner or put it off until tomorrow morning.

When Joe and Alex slipped into the dining room, they were just in time for dinner, having missed the optional cocktail hour because of a delay in

Alex's flight. As partners began to gravitate toward the tables, Joe walked Alex around the room, introducing him casually—just his name, firm, and city—to ten or so of the partners. Within a few minutes, Joe and Alex had drinks from the bar and had taken seats.

Since the round tables had been set for nine rather than eight, Joe could see at a glance, once everyone was seated, that there was only one laggard—Harold. This did not come as a surprise. Like so much else, Harold had come to regard the annual retreat as somewhat optional for one of his exalted state. He usually showed up at some point during the weekend, but even that wasn't set in stone. He had mentioned to Joe on Tuesday that he "might not be able to make it this year," mumbling something about a "family commitment." Joe had informed him, emphatically, that attendance at this retreat was mandatory, and Harold had shaken his head and said he'd see what he could do.

Perhaps reading Joe's thoughts, Alex leaned over and spoke softly. "Who're we missing?"

"Harold," Joe said with a sigh.

"Ah," Alex breathed. "Do you think he'll show up later?"

"Who the heck knows?" Joe said with irritation. "We had this conversation precisely two days ago. He said he might not be here; I told him he'd better. This is so infuriating!"

Heads were starting to turn in their direction, and Alex took a moment to reassure Joe. "Let it go," he said. "If he really doesn't show up—well, that information is just as important, maybe more so, than anything he could have said if he'd spent the whole weekend here. So just let it go."

Joe nodded with resignation and turned to Kevin, who was seated on his other side. "How was your drive over, Kevin? It's great having something like this so close to the city, isn't it? . . . "

An hour and a half later, Alex sat quietly, enormously reassured by what he'd seen this evening. Actually, he found that he'd been mentally holding his breath, which told him he'd formed an emotional investment already in this initiative. Sometimes it can be nice doing business with friends, he reflected.

The reason for his relief was simple. People who fundamentally dislike or mistrust each other have a highly dubious basis for shared enterprises. Major growth initiatives can be taxing enough to strain even strong working relationships, and Alex knew that without those strong bonds, they're often doomed before they start. Thus, the fact that these partners seemed genuinely to enjoy each other's company was a real plus.

Reassured, he tuned back in to conditions at his own table. Matthew Hanover and Smith Smoot both appeared mildly stunned to have ended up at a table with many of the firm's leaders—among them Joe, Eric, Charles, and Kevin. Kevin's voice broke through Alex's thoughts. It sounded as though he were repeating a question. "When're you guys planning to take the lid off?"

Alex noted that Joe looked mystified, and finally Eric stepped in. "I think he means the questionnaire results. You had to know that, right, Joe? There's more interest in the outcome of that one little poll. . . . Hey, everybody's buzzing about it, from the mailroom on up."

Joe chuckled. "That's hardly what we had in mind when we sent it around." He gestured toward his friend with a smile. "I think Alex is planning to open that up tomorrow morning, right, Alex?"

Alex made a quick decision: Why not start now? He shrugged and said, "No big mystery. You want the bad news or the good?" Then he grinned quickly and added, "Just kidding. Though in truth, there is a little bit of both. One thing we learned is that we have very strong performance in some of our niches. Right, Eric?"

Eric smiled, pleased to have been singled out. He launched eagerly into a description of the growth effort he'd spearheaded, the ideas he'd picked up at his niche meetings, how he'd tried to implement them at C&P. The discussion picked up steam as Kevin joined in, and then Alex turned to Smith and said, "I hear very good things about your work in business valuation. That's a real potential growth area for the firm."

The conversation moved along, and Joe sat back, basking in this moment of amity. He gazed around at his partners, scattered among the three tables, and experienced a moment of intense pride. These were good guys, by and large, these partners. They'd work with him to make a go of it.

Then Charles yawned ostentatiously and made a point of gazing conspicuously at his wristwatch. After a brief pause, the conversation at the table continued, but to Joe, it felt as if a giant cloud had just positioned itself overhead, blocking out the sun and its warmth. The glow of cognac and friendship was upon them right now, but tomorrow it would be different. Tomorrow morning Alex would empty the bag, and they'd all begin to see the long, bumpy road ahead. Would they agree to travel that road? Would they have the foresight to change, or would they choose to remain mired hopelessly in the past?

Joe shook his head slowly, trying to shake this feeling of foreboding. He'd soon know.

Sharpening the Knives

The partners strolled in, singly and in pairs and small groups. Some seemed a bit groggy; Joe knew that, according to long-established custom, several partners had closed down the bar the night before. There was some good-natured grumbling about being cooped up inside on such a glorious morning. They could have been outside playing golf!

All in all, though, Joe thought as he greeted the partners filing into the room, people seemed ready to dive in. The prevailing feeling seemed to be, *We're here, so why not make the best of it?*

Joe's pleasure was short lived. As Charles, the last to enter, was taking his place at the table, Frank Pierce piped up, "Where the heck is Harold? Isn't he supposed to be here too?"

Several partners glanced around as if searching for the missing partner, but there was no consternation. Ben Spencer joked, "I can't decide. Is this like Harold, or not? It *is* like him not to show if he doesn't feel like it. But it *isn't* like him to skip the one part of the job that doesn't require work."

There was subdued laughter, and then Charles raised his voice. "I thought attendance was mandatory. Who cares about these things less than I? and I'm here." Charles waved an arm dismissively. "Somebody get him on the phone."

Charles's gaze then fastened on Jackie, as if it were her duty to act as secretary. She glanced at Joe and saw a slight shake of his head. "We'll track him down, Charles," Joe said.

But then Kevin joined in. "I think Charles has a point. We're here, and Harold's supposed to be here too. I'll tell you frankly, Joe, that if there're changes to be made, that might be as good a place to start as any. What does it mean to be a partner in this firm? What are the obligations?"

"Harold doesn't care about obligations," Durwood said. "You know that. He cares about one year, three months . . . whatever the current countdown is to his retirement."

"If he wants to retire, and he doesn't want to do his part till then, then let him get on with it now," Kevin snapped.

"It's academic in the extreme, and you know that," Charles chided, abandoning his earlier position entirely. "Do you want him here just to get his goat? What could he possibly say—my goodness, what has he said in the last ten years—that you've paid the slightest notice to? This is just a sideshow."

"He's drawing a partnership percentage, and he's not holding up his end of the bargain," Kevin said ominously. "Joe made it clear how critical this meeting is, and it's of paramount importance to every member of this firm—to our personal bottom lines. And Harold can't bother to show up? Hey, either be a partner and act like one, or get out! I'd say it to his face if he'd bother to show it."

"Gentlemen," Alex said mildly as he arose. "If you please. This is hardly the way your managing partner"—with a nod to Joe, still seated by his side—"and I had intended to open this meeting, but it's an opportunity I hate to pass up. Let's talk about just that: what we're here for, where we're going, and who'll be coming along. I think you'll find the conversation very interesting."

Diving In

"Let me start, though, by thanking everyone for your thoughtful responses on the questionnaire. What we're going to be doing, over the next two days, is using those responses—*your* thoughts, *your* opinions—as a basis to evaluate and plan."

As Alex paused for breath, Frank's nasal tones broke through the momentary silence. "If that's true, if the responses to that questionnaire are the basis you intend to use, then I would argue that only the partners' responses should count. I don't think the staff should have been asked for their opinions anyway." Frank looked around him for support and saw a few heads nod in agreement. "After all, they don't have the experience to know where this firm needs to go."

"That makes sense," Alex said. "It is your firm, but think about it for a minute. When you're faced with a big decision, don't you try to gather *all* the information you can to help you make it?"

"Yes," Frank responded, "but for heaven's sake, Joe sent that thing out to *everybody*, including the mailroom clerks and the receptionist. Now what could a mailroom clerk possibly have to say that would help us make a decision?"

Joe, who'd seen the results of the questionnaire, had to bite his tongue to avoid saying, "Well, maybe that given the volume of non–business-related stuff that pours into our mailroom, he wonders how some of the partners find time to do any work. And the receptionist—she deals with clients who're stuck cooling their heels in the waiting room because partners are running late and didn't bother to call to let them know." He kept his silence, though, and let Alex handle it.

"I used to feel that way too," Alex said—though Joe knew that to be a polite fiction—"but then I found out that staff sometimes see us more clearly than we see ourselves. Out of the mouths of babes, right?"

"I don't agree," Frank said stiffly, but Alex broke in before he could launch into another diatribe.

"How about if we set that one aside for the time being, shall we? Let's start with our perspective." Alex then pressed on, pulling up the cover sheet on a large flipchart. "As Joe mentioned in his e-mail message, our objective for this retreat is to identify where we are as a firm, decide where we want to be in three years, and craft a strategy to get there. Make sense?" Heads nodded around the room. "Good. So today we're going to evaluate where we are, and to do that we'll use something called a SWOT analysis."

Joe was pleased to note that all eyes seemed to be focused on the flipchart. "On the left, here," Alex said, "you see two cells, labeled 'Strengths' and 'Opportunities.' On the right are two more, 'Weaknesses' and 'Threats.' Or we could look at it another way, top and bottom. The top line represents internal variables, and the bottom line is external variables. Everybody with me?" Heads nodded, and Alex went on . . .

Over the course of the next hour and a half, Alex led the Crandall & Potter partners in a spirited discussion that ranged over the full gamut of the firm's accomplishments and shortcomings, using the results from the questionnaire as a launching point.

Strengths that emerged from the questionnaire results centered around the fact that partners and staff alike perceived Crandall & Potter as an employee-friendly, family-friendly environment where morale was generally high. The benefits were generous, job security was good, and staff and younger partners alike believed there was room for career growth at C&P.

Alex read comments culled from the responses, using them as launching points for discussion. One partner had scribbled, "Joe's wife, Becky, bakes a cake every day during tax season, and brings it in to sustain the late-night tax warriors. (My wife wants to know if we can borrow her for a couple of weeks in December to help out with the Christmas baking!)" A young woman from the mailroom noted that the firm's summer picnic was always a grand affair, with catered food and drink, terrific decorations, plus loads of games and prizes. "I just love seeing these button-down pin-stripes doing the potato sack race," she'd written. "And, just like at the office, they all want to come in first!"

It was agreed that the firm had developed a reputation for strong technical competence, for delivering high-quality work, and for completing projects in a timely, professional manner. "This is terrific news," Alex said. "These are things that—some of them—can be next to impossible to fix. What do you do if your partners aren't up to snuff? That's the problem nobody wants to have, and you *don't* have it at Crandall & Potter. So congratulations on putting together a group of top-notch technicians."

But there was also the flip side, the shortcomings, and a short way into that discussion, Alex made a statement that caught everyone's attention. "Why do you think there's such a huge discrepancy between expectations and realities at Crandall & Potter?" Everyone seemed to grasp what he meant instinctively, and the discussion quickly grew vigorous.

"When Al Potter was here, you could count on double-digit growth every year, like clockwork," Frank complained.

"Come on, Frank," Kevin said. "Be fair. Our base was smaller then— much smaller, in the earlier years."

"That may be true," Durwood put in, "but it's not the whole story. I was talking with Eric last week and . . . What were those growth figures you were quoting, Eric?"

"Good point, Durwood," Alex said, stepping in smoothly to reassert control over the discussion. "And we'll get to that exact issue—growth— very shortly. But first let's finish looking at this issue of expectations and realities. Who wants to take a shot at listing some places where C&P has been falling short here?"

Eric decided to put his oar in. "Well," he said, "if you set aside the issue of growth per se, there's still the *effect* it has, in limiting the partners' potential for professional development. As partners, we can try to hack out our own path, but that kind of situation can feel pretty chaotic."

Matthew, the youngest member of the firm, decided to take the leap by voicing a concern he'd had nearly the whole time he'd been at C&P. "I think Eric's onto something," he said. "It's like there's no common vision here, like everybody's doing their own thing, with no rhyme or reason. And a young partner like me—hey, I want to make good, I want to do well at Crandall & Potter. But where do I land; how do I make that decision? Do I figure out on my own which niche to pursue? And how to pursue it?"

"I think Matt's right," Kevin cut in abruptly. "And I've thought so for a long time. It's the industries we're in—there're too darn many of them, and they don't make sense as a whole. It's like every single partner says, 'Hey, here's a lead in construction—sounds good to me,' and off they go chasing it, and then next week it's medical device manufacturing, or some fool thing, and who knows what the week after that? There's no plan—as Matt said, no rhyme or reason. I feel like we woke up one day and realized that we have no common client profile. Every lead has been a good lead, whether it played to our strengths or not."

"So what're you saying, Kevin?" Durwood asked. "If I get a good lead in a niche we're not already in, I'm supposed to ignore it? How are we ever going to grow with that attitude?"

Alex stood back and let the conversation take its course for several minutes, observing the ebb and flow as partners kicked the question around. Finally he decided to step back in. "You know, you're all right on some level," he said. "If I were to summarize, I'd say that we need to pursue leads in new fields to keep growth robust, but when we chase every lead willy nilly, that does end in chaos. And the conflict between the two approaches—chase all leads versus try to impose discipline—runs throughout the responses we got back.

"It's not just Crandall & Potter, by the way; this is a question every firm has to face as it maps out its plan for growth. The conflict and ambivalence you all feel—it's real, and we'll grapple with it plenty over the next two days. After all, isn't that why we're here?"

To Grow or Not to Grow?

"All right," Alex went on after the break. "We have an apparent contradiction here. On the one hand, it seems like we chase every lead we hear about, whether it's a strategic fit or not. On the other hand, we can see that that's not working, because we don't have strong, sustained growth.

"But here's another part of the equation: How effective are we in going after new leads? Who wants to tackle that one first?"

As he had earlier, Alex led the partners through this discussion, drawing them out, eliciting observations, inviting counterarguments, then doubling back to synthesize and invite still more comments. Through it all, he wove results from the questionnaire skillfully into the discussion, reminding them that they had at hand powerful firsthand evidence of where they actually were as a firm. The only remaining issue, then, was to decide, first, where they truly wanted to be and, second, how to get there.

"But we *aren't growing*," Kevin said insistently, leaning forward on the table. "Our whole profession is taking off, growing like wildfire, and we grew, what?, seven percent last year. And what did you tell me last week, Joe? That that's mostly *price increases*, nothing more. It's not nearly good enough."

"Well, why was that the case?" Alex asked. "Why don't we take another look at the questionnaire responses?" He picked up a notebook, found his place quickly, and looked up. "You know, this is very interesting. This is one of several places where staff saw things very differently from partners. *You* all"—gesturing to the partners in attendance—"generally say you're pursuing leads in a focused manner. Staff tends to see it differently.

"Let's listen to some of their comments. Here's one: 'Everybody's got their own pet project, and nobody ever sets any priorities. It's a constant free-for-all, and it seems like there's never any overall plan.' Another response says, 'The partners are always running around in a hundred different directions. All leads are good leads.'" Alex looked up. "Does that feel familiar?"

The partners weighed in again, some arguing that pet projects aren't all bad and that all leads *should* be followed up regardless of size or fit, and others believing an overarching strategy would be a welcome change, though it might feel uncomfortable at first.

Alex allowed that conversation to develop, then steered things subtly to a discussion of delivery versus business development. "Here's one comment that suggests an explanation for the lack of growth. It says the audit, tax, and other department leaders spend all their time on delivery issues, overseeing quality control, methodologies, and resource deployment, and so have no time to focus on business development and the growth of their services. Kevin, what's your gut response to that?''

Alex had chosen Kevin because he knew the tax guru was serious about growth, and he wanted to draw him into consideration of the nitty-gritty issues. Kevin reddened slightly, but then began nodding his head slowly. "I think there's probably a lot of truth in that. I wonder, though, if it's only a matter of priorities. I wonder if maybe we focus on delivery because that's what we know how to do, and going after new business is less comfortable, or maybe even familiar, to a lot of us."

Several people jumped in immediately, and Alex let the conversation proceed before he made his next comment. "There's support in these responses for what Kevin saw instinctively," he said. "Listen to this comment, from somebody who's obviously an old-timer: 'Lots of these partners are second-generation guys. They never had to go out and hunt up business, so they don't know how.' "

There was a spontaneous burst of laughter around the table, and Joe clued Alex in: "We all know who that is: Thaddeus Cox. He's as old as Methuselah, and he's been running the mailroom since it took deliveries from the Pony Express." Joe shook his head, offering one of his few observations to date. "He's probably got a point. Maybe we're all so comfortable that we don't even know *how* to be hungry."

"*I* know how to be hungry," Matthew burst out, "I just don't know how to *hunt*." The laughter that greeted this comment was even heartier than before, and Matthew looked slightly defensive, so Alex moved to rescue him. "Well put, Matthew. And I can guarantee that you're not the only one. Not to jump ahead, but let me put your mind at rest. One of the things we're going to be doing, not today but over the next few months, is figuring out who's a rainmaker and who wants to be, and then teaching the ones who *want* to be, how to be. Good enough?"

Matthew nodded, grateful and relieved.

As they moved toward the lunch break, Alex pulled one more surprise out of his hat. "We're going to try to nail this down," he said as he walked around the room, handing a slip of paper to each participant. "Take a minute or two to think about it, and then write down exactly how much you want Crandall & Potter to grow annually over the next three years.

"No names, please, and no other information, just the percentage. When you're finished, fold the slips and drop them here on your way out." He smiled as he watched the partners' faces crease in thought.

It seemed to Joe that the group reassembled more quickly than usual; there seemed to be a palpable sense of eagerness to hear the results of Alex's straw poll. "Well, here's where we are," he began. "The lowest desired growth number was 5 percent, even lower than C&P experienced last year." Joe could hear a few gasps and groans, and a couple of partners opened their mouths to speak, but Alex held up a hand. "On the other end of the range, we have two respondents who'd like to see 20-percent growth." This time there were several whistles and more than a few thoughtful nods. "The rest of the responses fall somewhere in between; there was no single number that drew a significant number of responses.

"What this tells me is that the undercurrent I heard running through the discussion earlier this morning is in fact the reality—there's no consensus at all on this point.

"But that's okay," he went on. "That's what this meeting is for—part of it, anyway." Having gained the partners' full attention, Alex then launched into an analysis of the reasons behind their widely diverging responses.

"Here's what you need to understand," Alex explained. "At the beginning, it's natural for everybody to have a different idea of how much growth the firm should shoot for. Each person's view has a lot to do with their vision of what growth will do for them individually, not necessarily what it will do for the firm.

"But that's not necessarily about selfishness," he hastened to add. "You think that way because, like most firms, you started with a 'book of business' model—you ate what you killed, so to speak. So it's pretty much automatic. If you're an older partner, more comfortable, more secure, you're likely to favor a more conservative approach, and maybe you won't see the need to pour a lot of resources into making the firm grow. For the younger partners, it's a whole different ball game. They might be fondest of growth plans that'll give the biggest boost to their career path. With perspectives that are so diverse, the good of the whole firm becomes an afterthought.

"And here's another consideration—one that may not even have occurred to you before. What about the future of Crandall & Potter as an entity? When you current partners retire, what will you be leaving to the ones who come after you?"

Alex gave this question a moment to sink in, then went on. "Who in this room just wants to take the money and run?" He paused for a show of hands, but of course saw none. "Who has no desire to hand this firm over to the next generation even stronger than you found it?" Again, Alex paused for a moment for effect, but this time Ben broke the silence.

"If Harold were here, you'd have a taker!" he said, and the room rang with laughter.

"So I've heard," Alex said, joining in with a chuckle, "but the rest of you feel that sense of responsibility, that fiduciary duty to the future of your firm. And that's a good thing, an honorable thing." (Later, Alex would explain to Joe how crucial the buy-in on this concept was, because this was the lever that would pry many partners out of their complacency, enable them to see beyond their own W-2 earnings. With strategic reminders, the concept would ultimately provide the impetus these partners needed to forge a commitment to grow with the rest of their profession.)

"So again," Alex stressed, "different aims come not from bad intentions, but as a natural response. So the challenge for people at both ends of the spectrum—and for everybody in the middle as well, of course—is to let go of what I'll call a 'me-centric' view of growth, in order to explore what's good for the firm as a whole.

"When you *don't* have that suspension of 'mecentric' thinking—and you can't suspend it until you know how—you get exactly what we find reflected in these questionnaire responses: lots of conflict and ambivalence about growth. So, as we try to feel our way toward a strategic plan"—Alex paused as Charles snorted audibly—"we need to keep a few key issues in mind. Namely, one, where are we now? Two, where do we want to be? And three, what do we have to do to get there?"

As Alex ticked off the points, Joe took a moment to glance around the room. He was pleased to see many heads nodding in agreement, though Charles looked skeptical and Frank's face bore a pained look Joe couldn't even label. He turned his attention back to Alex.

"Specifically, then, our strategy development will be informed by our vision and mission, and we'll start by defining specific goals and objectives. But before we dive into that . . . " Alex paused and took a moment to move his eyes around the room. "I want to touch on another issue, one that's critically important, though it seems you all don't realize it.

"Aside from the partners in this firm, your two best resources for growth are your marketing director and your business developer. What I want to know is this," Alex said. "Why are those two people, who are so essential to your firm's long-term success . . . Why aren't they here?"

The First Sticky Wicket

There was a stir as several partners shuffled their feet or some papers, but no one seemed eager to speak. Joe opened his mouth, but Alex motioned subtly for him to wait.

After a pause that lasted a full minute, Charles spoke up in a petulant tone. "They aren't here because they weren't invited. And they weren't invited because the annual retreat is for *partners*. They're staff, and that's all there is to it. After all, rank has to have its privileges *sometimes*."

"You know, that's a good point, Charles," Alex said, much to Joe's surprise. "In the past, at least, that logic made good sense. This retreat used to be pretty much a perk, a weekend golf holiday, if you will, that the partners gave each other, and themselves, as a reward for another year's hard work.

"But we're doing something different this year, and I always believe that change can start with the very words we use. So I suggest that we start by changing what we call this annual retreat. I propose that we rechristen it the strategic summit. How does that sound?"

Joe could sense puzzlement in the room; he was afraid the partners might feel that they'd been caught off balance twice. First Alex had brought up the issue of the missing staffers, and then he'd compounded it by dragging in the issue of the retreat's name. Joe felt a bit off balance himself.

"All right, I admit that wasn't fair," Alex said with a laugh. "Let's back up and take things one at a time. First, the name for this yearly get-together. When I hear the word 'retreat,' I think of, oh, time away from the bustle and hurry of the world, time for calm and reflection, meditation perhaps. Very laid back. Agreed?

"But is that what we're here for? No, we're here to work and plan, to map out a strategy that'll move us forward aggressively in our field. We're not here to reflect and meditate, we're here to forge a competitive strategy. Why not use words that express our intentions?

"Any thoughts?"

There was a pause, and then Kevin's voice: "What was that name you mentioned, Alex?"

"'Strategic summit.' That's what we call our annual getaway at Weinstein & Federman. What do you think, Kevin?"

"I suppose it makes sense," Kevin said, rubbing his chin doubtfully. "It'll take some getting used to, that's for sure."

"Words are powerful tools," Alex said. "Don't ever forget that. The labels we give things do affect the way we think about them. I want you all to start thinking of this yearly meeting as your supreme planning time."

"Works for me," Eric said, and, looking around, he noticed several nods of agreement.

"Done," Alex said. "Now, on to that other issue, and this is about seeing things clearly as well. We're not here to play golf, we're here to work and plan and map out the strategy that will guide this firm over the next twelve months to three years. How can you afford to have your marketing director and business developer absent?"

"If you knew them, you might not ask," Frank cracked. Joe shook his head, embarrassed by the guilty laughter the comment elicited.

"Really," Alex said. "Tell me why."

Frank replied immediately. "It's very simple, Alex. Our marketing director's an airhead, and our business developer's a playboy. Neither of 'em's worth a plugged nickel."

"Now wait a minute," Eric put in. "That's really unfair. Tiff has had some terrific ideas, and she works as hard as anybody in this firm. Have you seen the marketing awards she's picked up for the work she's done for us? When was the last time you were even in her office?"

"Probably the day the fire inspector dropped by to condemn it as a fire hazard," Frank shot back. "Her office always looks like a bomb just went off."

Alex had cautioned Joe to stay out of these little frays, to let them develop as they would. So he sat silently as Smith, of all people, leapt to Tiff's defense. "The brochures she's made up are the nicest this firm has ever had. They're beautiful. And so is the Web site. Tiff has a real eye for design."

"I agree that the Web site's well designed," Ben put in, "but it's also constantly out of date. She may have good ideas, but I don't think organization is her long suit."

"At least she's been willing to hang in there with us," Durwood said. "This is the—what?—the third marketing director we've had, and nobody else lasted longer than two or three years. The one before her chucked it in after nine months, as I recall, and went back to an ad agency."

The partners continued to kick Tiff back and forth, but little consensus emerged. Some partners liked her work, while others had no idea whatsoever what her role even was. There did seem to be a general sense that marketing efforts were pursued haphazardly, that there was no over-riding sense of direction.

"But that's true of the firm as a whole, isn't it?" Alex said pointedly. "Now, how about the other half of that tandem?"

"Right, Tiff'n'Ty, Tiff'n'Ty, Tiff'n'Ty," Charles recited in a singsong voice. "It's fitting that we discuss them together, because it often seems to me that they're attached at the hip."

Amid general laughter, Eric plunged in. "Ty means well, but I often get the feeling that he's out of his depth with us."

There were thoughtful nods around the room, and Joe was hoping the conversation would stay on this plane when Frank held forth once again. "That's awfully generous, Eric. I'd have to say, too generous." Frank shifted his attention to Alex and let go. "Have you met this specimen? He wears a *pinkie ring*, for heaven's sake!"

Alex tried to defuse the situation. "Well, he certainly has made an impression on you, Frank. Granted that presentation is important, that looks count, what is it about his actual job performance that leaves you cold?"

Frank seemed to sense that he might have stepped over a line and tried to retreat into what was, for him, civility. "He brings nothing to the table, Alex. Nothing. For instance, when we had that first meeting to discuss the pipeline inventory Joe had Jackie put together—"

"I don't mean to interrupt you, Frank, but there's an important point about terminology here," Alex said. "Not pipeline inventory, just 'pipeline.'" He pulled back from Frank to take in the entire group. "Does that make sense to everybody? We keep track of our projects in the *pipeline*, and we update the *pipeline* as we go along. It's not a pipeline list or a pipeline inventory or a pipeline report or a pipeline anything, just a *pipeline*. Okay?

"Oh, and one more thing. When we get together to talk about what's in the pipeline, we call that a pipeline *review*, not a pipeline meeting, which I've also heard once or twice. So we've got the *pipeline* and the pipeline *review*. Pipeline. Pipeline review. Got it?"

Heads nodded, and Alex motioned to Frank to continue. "Okay. The pipeline Jackie put together."

"Yes," Frank said. "So we went through everybody's leads, all the partners', and then here comes Ty with his own list of . . . his own *pipeline*. Remember, Joe?"

Joe nodded, dolefully aware of what had to be coming. "Well, you never saw such nonsense," Frank groused. "How many companies did Ty have on his . . . pipeline, Joe?"

Joe shrugged his shoulders. "About twenty, I think."

"Right," Frank said. "And how many were left when we got finished going through 'em?"

"Maybe a couple," Joe admitted, though he knew even that was stretching it.

"Right!" Frank hissed, aiming a finger at Alex. "Because his 'leads' were all worthless! And the plans he had for 'developing' them! I'll tell you, Ty Dukes has no more idea what to do with a prospect than my granddaughter does. All he knows is, Play golf with 'em, take 'em to lunch, or buy 'em tickets to a football game!

"And I'll tell you something else: He comes across like a lightweight. I mean, he talks about himself in the third person, for crying out loud! He calls himself 'the Ty Guy.' The Ty Guy! How can you expect us to go out on calls with someone who's liable to come out with something like, 'The Ty Guy knows just where you're coming from.' It's humiliating, and I won't do it!"

"At the considerable risk of siding with Frank," Kevin said wryly, "and laying aside the issue of Ty's curious means of expression, I think Frank has some valid points. I'd say Ty has a couple of weaknesses. One is that he doesn't seem to know how to bring new business in on his own. My guess is that he's worked his way through his Rolodex, and he doesn't know what to do next.

"The second thing is that, in terms of providing support for us as we go after new clients, it just seems like there's not much there—much substance. He's long on style, as Frank pointed out—his clothes are terrific, and he drives a fancy little sports car—but that seems to be about it."

"And he's a playboy!" Frank added, thrusting his hand out dramatically.

"I don't think we know that," Kevin said.

"I'm not sure we need to," Alex said. "Because I think we're getting ahead of ourselves. We're going to look very closely at these two staff functions later, but right now I want to get back to the issue we started with—the fact that Tiff and Ty should be here, and aren't. We're going to get this one settled, once and for all."

Some Tough Talk from Alex

"It's really not very complicated," Alex went on. "Here's the bottom line: Marketing and business development are two key functions, vital to future growth at Crandall & Potter. I understand from Joe that he made clear how important it was to have Tiff and Ty here, but nearly half the partners raised a stink about it anyway.

"So let me speak directly to those individuals right now. This is not about your egos, it's about driving disciplined practice growth. Having key people on hand at the yearly strategy session is nothing more or less than *proper business practice*. And it should be abundantly clear that that's far more important than protecting some outdated pecking order."

He stopped and gave his words time to sink in. "Is that clear enough? And does anyone want to dispute the point, or think we need further discussion on the matter?"

After a few moments had passed, he said, "All right. And on that note, I think we'll break for lunch." As Alex turned his back on the partners to gather his things and go, he knew he'd looked and sounded harsh. He didn't care. These people needed to get the message loud and clear. The age of genteel collegiality was over. It was time to get serious.

To show that there were no hard feelings left over from the morning, Alex launched the afternoon session with a smile. On the table at everyone's place was a brochure called "Guide to Strategic Planning." The brochures were all opened to a page called "Developing Your Firm's Vision Statement/Mission Statement/Core Values."

"This is where it gets real," Alex said by way of introduction. "Our aim is to develop a three-year plan, so what things do we need to consider as we do so? I've found it useful to follow a model developed by a Kansas company called Boomer Consulting.[1] I'd like you to take a few moments to look at their piece."

After pausing, Alex went on. "You'll see that everything flows from the key issue of the company's vision. The vision, once defined, makes it possible to delineate a mission, and that in turn informs a set of core values, a strategic plan, and the core processes necessary to implement the plan."

At this point, Charles sighed audibly, and Alex decided to tackle his resistance on the spot. "You may not see it now, Charles," he said, "but if you'll trust me on this, I think it'll start making sense pretty shortly."

Charles was surprised that Alex had challenged him, but decided to respond. "We're CPAs, Alex," Charles said, "not a bunch of social workers. Do we really need a 'mission'? Our mission is to practice our profession and make money, for crying out loud. We don't need some mumbo jumbo to show us how to do that."

"Isn't part of your mission keeping pace in your profession?" Alex countered. "C&P hasn't been doing that lately. If it had been, I wouldn't be here now."

Charles swallowed hard and retreated slightly. He flipped through the brochure and seized on a heading at random. " 'Integrity and Honesty.' " He snorted. "Do you really think we have work to do there? Come on!" He gesticulated broadly, at the same time glancing around for signs of support.

"No, I don't think that's a problem area," Alex said equably. "But another item on that list is 'Client Relationships.' Then there's 'Respect and Teamwork.' How have you all been doing in those areas lately?

"And how about 'Preparedness'? Joe told me that in your first pipeline review, you learned that two of you were working up bids for the same new client, and neither of you knew about the other. You were competing against yourselves! So I'd say there are some gaps to be filled there too."

---

[1]Boomer Consulting, Inc. "The Guide to Strategic Planning," (2003). Manhattan, Kansas.

Charles looked down, shaking his head. Alex knew Charles wasn't persuaded, but he turned to address his comments to the entire room. "Let me say, to all of you who may share Charles's reservations, that what I'm talking about here is not touchy-feely, it is brass tacks. This is the *nuts and bolts* of putting together a plan and then making sure you can follow through. All I ask is that you keep an open mind; it'll make more sense as we go along."

"What we're looking for," Alex continued, "is a set of guiding principles that, taken together, define the way we go about our work. Then we check to make sure we have the machinery in place to support those principles. Boomer calls this 'alignment'—making sure the nuts and bolts of your operation are in line with your firm's stated goals." Alex paused. "Those of you who are really interested in this can find more about it on their Web site, Boomer.com."

He turned back to his main subject. "Some of these things are already in place here; we talked about them earlier when we discussed the firm's strengths—things like technical excellence, reliability, and professionalism. But there are others we'll want to add. Once this is all in place, we'll be able to set specific goals and objectives, then define the critical factors that will both help and hinder our efforts to achieve them. Last, we'll map out specific plans of action.

"You see, it really is very nuts and bolts." Alex looked directly at Charles and was rewarded with a slight, grudging nod.

Alex stepped to his flipchart and quickly sketched out six boxes, two on the top row, three in the middle, and one on the bottom. "We're going to get into this much more tomorrow, but I want to give you a quick sense of it right now. These top two boxes are, let's say, the current guiding principles of Crandall & Potter." Alex filled in the two boxes on top, writing "Get Out There" on the left and "Do Good Work" on the right. "This is your formula, developed by Albert Potter and followed faithfully since the firm's early days.

"It was a formula that brought success in the old days, and it kept right on working for a long time. But at some point the ground shifted, and, unfortunately, Crandall & Potter didn't shift with it.

"Now, speaking generally, practice growth efforts today fall into four categories, and I'll sketch them in for you." Alex turned and filled in the middle three boxes: Marketing on the left, Industry Niche Management in the middle, and Large Opportunity Management to the right. In the lone box on the bottom row, he wrote Service Line Management.

"Let's look, now, at the current Crandall & Potter approach to these four—let's call them levers. The four levers:

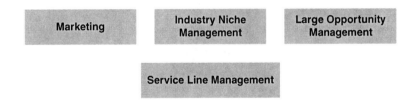

"First we have marketing, and what have we concluded about that effort? Mainly that marketing in its current incarnation is a tactical toolbox, nothing more. There's no real vision, and no one seems very clear about what Tiff's role is.

"Second, industry niche management. Here we've found that the approach to niches is haphazard at best. There is one real success story—Eric in health care—but none of the other niches are growing. And I think we'll find, when we delve into that discussion, that Eric's been doing some very specific things to achieve that success. In general, there's no strategic direction in this area, and certainly there's no muscle behind it.

"Third, we have large opportunity management; here the approach is entirely without focus. Joe told me about that huge prospect that fell by the boards in large part because of a lack of coordination. We'll get to that one later. But for now, it suffices to say that your business developer should be working hand in glove with all the partners to keep your efforts here focused and on target, and that is not what's happened."

Alex paused for breath. "Finally, service line management, a lever that for all intents and purposes does not exist at Crandall & Potter. This is where strategic direction should be concentrated, with segment leaders responsible for crafting strategic direction and overseeing the financial health of service lines. Instead, the focus is entirely on delivery, with absolutely nothing on the growth side of the ledger.

"Now," Alex concluded, "as we go through the rest of the afternoon, I want you to keep these levers in mind at all times. This is where we'll find our answers; these are the four keys to disciplined growth, and I want us to start getting used to thinking along these lines. Who wants to be first?"

Best Practices and More

After some initial hesitation, the partners got into the spirit of the discussion, and when they wandered from the framework Alex had set, he gently drew them back in. He continued to make liberal use of the questionnaire responses and encouraged partners to be as specific as they could in their comments.

As Alex had suggested, there were some surprises, and the conversation occasionally grew testy. Alex opened the discussion about industry niche management by noting the nearly 20-percent growth the previous year in the health care niche and asking Eric how he'd gotten those terrific results.

"That's obvious," Frank cut in. "Health care's growing by leaps and bounds these days."

Eric shot a look of annoyance at the older partner, but Alex stepped in before he could reply. "Really?" he said. "Market conditions, hmm? Well, one of the biggest growth segments for accounting as a whole last year was real estate. That's your niche, I believe. How much growth did your segment see last year?"

Frank reddened but did not respond. "I'll let you off the hook," Alex said shortly, "and we'll go ahead and let Eric answer my question."

Eric replied that he'd been meeting with a group of CPAs focused on health care and implementing an approach—he described it briefly— he'd learned from others in the group. "Excellent," Alex said when Eric had finished. "That's precisely the point—it's not just market conditions, it's *best practices.* What Eric's been learning at these meetings of his is *product management best practices,* and he's put them in place here with great success. Can you fill that in a bit more, Eric? Give us some more specifics?"

Joe smiled as the other partners listened intently to his protégé's enthusiastic description of the new approach he'd learned.

As the group moved on to address each of the four levers, Alex summarized the group's findings on his flipchart. Jake Billings got the discussion about service line management going by saying, "If we're talking about segments, mine is litigation support. What exactly does that make me responsible for?"

"Are you the leader in this segment?" Alex asked.

"I think so," Jake responded, and Joe nodded in confirmation.

"Well, that makes you the segment leader, and that means that you're responsible for the strategic direction and financial health of litigation support. Here's what we'll be working toward: identifying leaders in each service line or industry, helping those leaders enhance their current offerings and develop new ones within the segment, developing metrics to track growth, providing incentives tied to performance, and, ulti- mately, of course, increasing revenue in each service line or industry."

"Sounds like a tall order," Jake said.

"It won't happen overnight," Alex assured him. "And you'll have lots of training; you won't be dropped on your head, I promise."

"You know," Kevin said, "one thread I hear running through everything that comes up is the lack of focus, or vision, if you will. But isn't that just another way of saying leadership, a lack of leadership? Alex, you've quoted from those questionnaire results so often they must be tattooed on your brain. What did people have to say about the leadership we have in place?"

Alex gulped mentally, but outwardly his demeanor didn't change. This was the part of the discussion he'd been looking forward to least, as he knew it would hurt his friend Joe. There was no avoiding it, though, so he jumped right in.

"Terrific question, Kevin," he began, reaching for his notes. "You've put your finger on one of the areas that needs fixing first. Here's what people said: Among partners, the feeling was strong that there's no common vision, no driving force that unites you as a group. Some of you found that more troubling than others, but many of you brought it up.

"Beyond that, there was a sense that the managing partner needs to do a better job of grooming leaders—that while the firm as a whole has lots of technical whizzes, it's a ship without a rudder. From the partner point of view, that's the situation in a nutshell.

"But . . . " Alex allowed the pause to stretch out for a moment, then went on. "Not everybody saw it that way, at least not in such black-and-white terms. A number of people said Joe's role has never been adequately defined. One said it's difficult to assess his leadership skills because the group of partners he's leading may not want to be led. 'Leading this group would be like herding cats,' this person wrote.

"Well." Alex looked up from his papers and smiled. "I invite you to spend this time here proving this person wrong. We'll see if we can't find a vision we can all agree on and a way to line up behind our managing partner."

The room emptied out for the afternoon break, with many partners surprised to see that the session had run far longer than expected. They'd been meeting for more than three hours straight, and nobody had gotten bored!

Alex stood to one side, talking with Joe. "Don't take it so hard," he said. "This is nothing we didn't already know, and it's nothing we can't fix."

"Yeah, but, remember, I looked at all the responses," Joe said. "I read the things that you, mercifully, didn't share—like 'He couldn't lead his way out of a paper bag'—"

"Obviously Frank," Alex broke in.

"Yeah, probably, but there was more; maybe nothing else quite that bald. These guys really think I'm letting them down; they don't think I've been cutting the mustard since Old Man Potter died."

"I'd say that's overstating things a good deal," Alex said. "But I have to warn you that the worst is still to come. Tonight, with the executive committee, we're going to tackle the idea of making you a full-time MP and paying you on that alone."

"At least Frank won't be there." Joe sighed.

"Why don't you try to suspend judgment, at least for a while," Alex coaxed. "You know, in your heart, that there's a kernel of truth in some of the comments. You haven't been the strongest leader—both because you've been a good consensus builder and because they didn't truly want you to lead. At some point, consensus building can work not only for you but against you.

"We're going to try to effect a change on both counts—your ability to lead and theirs to follow. So try to give them—and yourself—a chance. Feel the frustration, but then let it go. We can make this thing work, Joe, but a lot of it rests on you, and your attitude."

Ty Takes It on the Chin

"We ran long before the break, so this session will be a short one. Fortunately, there's only one box we haven't addressed," Alex began once they'd reassembled. He had headed into this final afternoon session feeling strong, buoyed by Joe's assurance that he was ready to move forward without reservation.

"That box, of course, is large opportunity management, and, while our discussion now will be brief, this is an area where I think there are some real issues. The questionnaire responses bear that out, and I've heard a lot of horror stories from you all directly. Stories like the time C&P lost a large prospect, and it turned out Joe knew the president of the company, but he didn't find out about the proposal until it was lost. The time—this came up at your last pipeline review—when Jake was chasing a lead, Medico, and didn't know till that meeting that Kevin was related to the controller there. Jake never would've found out, except for that meeting. Or—and I mentioned this one before—the time two partners were chasing the same prospect, both blissfully unaware that they were competing against themselves.

"How do these things happen? More important, how do we make them stop? Who's got an idea?"

Smith spoke up. "You mentioned one of the biggest ways, Alex. We talk to each other. Keep track of prospects in the pipeline and trade information."

"Good answer," Alex said. "But is there one individual who bears primary responsibility in this area?"

"I suppose that would be Ty," Eric said reluctantly.

"Right, your business developer," Alex replied. "Now, without turning this into character assassination time, can someone tell me, briefly, how Ty has or hasn't been measuring up?"

As the conversation developed, Ty's shortcomings were trotted forth and examined. It appeared that he worked closely with only a few of the partners, and even those individuals were hard pressed to make much of a case for him. It seemed he was seldom on hand when critical presentations were made to the largest and most strategically significant prospects.

"Is this his fault, or yours?" Alex asked bluntly. "Do you give him a chance with these heavy hitters?"

"That's a fair question," Kevin said, "and I think the answer is, probably, no, we don't. But I also think there's a reason for that. When you *do* bring Ty in, you find yourself afterward asking *why*. At least that's been my experience."

There were nods around the room, and Alex focused his attention on a partner who'd drawn his eye throughout the day. "Have you worked with him, Matthew?"

Matthew nodded. "I have, a few times. I'll tell you, it seems like he talks a good game—you know, he's full of enthusiasm and what I call happy talk—but clients aren't impressed with that. He's always complaining that we don't pull him in often enough, and I'll admit that I'm as guilty as the next guy. But you have to believe he's going to make a difference to go to the trouble. And to be honest, I haven't found that to be the case."

"It sounds like we have a consensus on this one," Alex said. "But I don't want to lay it all at Ty's door. Earlier this month, Crandall & Potter lost a huge opportunity, and I want to do a quick postmortem on that before we break for the evening. Charles, I believe that was your baby."

Charles had been all but napping, his chin in his hand, but he snapped to attention when he heard his name. "Yes?" he said vaguely, hoping Alex would repeat what he'd said.

"Your big tuna," Alex said. "The one that got away. Tell us about it."

Charles's face grew hot, but he told himself he had nothing to be ashamed of. "There's not a great deal to tell," he began. "We had what I thought was a terrific opportunity, an audit and tax engagement that we bid very aggressively on, and it seems we came very close to landing it. At the last minute, though, we lost it on price."

"Did you bring Ty in on it?"

"Be serious," Charles said, flicking a piece of imaginary lint from his sleeve.

"All right then. Did you bring *Kevin* in? It was audit and *tax*, you said, right?"

"No, I did not," Charles said, feeling the blood rise in his cheeks once more.

"It was a one-man show, then, is that it?" Alex let the pause lengthen, then addressed the whole group again. "We'll let Charles off the hook now. But there's a valuable lesson to be learned here—several of them, in fact. To be successful with larger opportunities, you must work together. Take advantage of *all* the resources of your firm."

He turned back to Charles. "Why did you lose out?"

"Price," Charles answered shortly.

"That seems to happen to us a lot," Ben observed.

"It does," Alex said, "when you aren't able to qualify properly and build a compelling value proposition in the mind of the prospect."

Alex laid his marker down and smiled. "That's about it for today, lady and gentlemen. To this point, we've been examining the problem, but tomorrow we get to the good part. Tomorrow we start on the solution."

As the partners filed from the room, Alex signaled to Eric, Kevin, and Charles. "This last session was short, so will a half-hour break do it? We've got a lot to tackle in the executive committee meeting."

Joe tried to stifle a sinking sensation inside. He had a feeling that *he* was the one who was going to wind up feeling tackled.

So Long, Farewell

"I'd like to thank Alex for agreeing to sit in with us," Joe began, after he, Kevin, Charles, and Eric had reassembled.

"Do you think this meeting will run very long, Alex?" Charles cut in plaintively. "It's been a long day already, and we have tomorrow's sessions ahead of us and then a drive back to the city. I'm sure we'd all appreciate it if we can keep this as short as possible."

Joe felt his muscles tense, but Alex appeared smooth and unruffled. "I really can't guarantee that, Charles," he said evenly. "In fact, I'll be completely truthful with you and say that brevity is the very least of my concerns. We have some issues to tackle that will have a vital effect on the long-term fortunes of Crandall & Potter. If you feel you can't give this meeting your full attention, then I'm sure I speak for the others when I say we'll be more than willing to excuse you."

Charles flushed, but tried to retain some dignity. "Not at all," he murmured stiffly.

Alex smiled cryptically and turned his attention back to the group. "Let's first map out the list of things we have to grapple with. Suggestions?"

"Tiff'n'Ty," Eric offered, sighing.

"Harold," Kevin added gruffly.

"Yes, those seem to be the pressing issues, plus one more that I'll bring up a bit later. So let's start with the two staffers, and what say we take Ty first. It looks like he may be the easier of the two."

"I think we pretty much said it all back there," Kevin began. "You heard the same things I did: He works with very few partners, and even those guys don't really think he's much help. He doesn't know what to do other than call up people from his prospect list, and that list ran dry a long time ago."

Eric took up the indictment. "It does seem that his efforts are largely confined to taking people out to eat or to the ball game—or sending them there on our dime."

Kevin leaned forward in his seat, thrusting his hand forward and screwing up his face in an uncanny imitation of Frank. "And he's a playboy!" he sang out. Everyone, even Charles, laughed heartily, and the mood perceptibly lightened.

Still smiling, Alex directed a question at Joe. "In that pipeline review, Frank mentioned that Ty came in with his own pipeline. Did it amount to much?"

"Not at all," Joe said truthfully. "It was a laundry list of wannabe prospects. When we went through it, there was nothing there. Not a single real lead, as I recall."

"He's been here how long?" Alex asked.

"Just over a year," Joe replied.

"All right, then, how shall we handle this? Suggestions?"

Kevin shook his head in frustration. "I guess we can him. I hate to just ax the guy, but what other choice do we have?"

For the next half hour, the executive committee wrestled with the inevitable. Finally Joe turned to Alex and said, "I guess that's it. It looks like we have a consensus that he has to go."

"Is Minnesota an at-will employment state?" Alex asked.

"It is," Joe replied.

"All right. Then you just provide whatever severance package you normally offer at that level."

Joe shifted uncomfortably in his chair. "We've never fired a senior staff member before."

"Okay," Alex said evenly, "then let's tackle that issue—specifics of the severance package."

"What do you do at Weinstein & Federman?" Eric asked.

Alex outlined their policy, and it was quickly embraced by the C&P executive committee.

"Now, for the difficult part," Alex said. "Who gets to do the honors?"

"Well," Joe said, "I hired him, so I think it's my responsibility to tell him he's gone."

Tiff was next on the grill, and here the partners found the going much less clear. "I can't argue with part of what Frank said," Joe began. "She is disorganized, and it's true that the Web site is constantly out of date. On the other hand, Eric's points were valid, too. She *has* won a boatload of awards for creative marketing ideas. Still, something tells me, after seeing Katherine in action, that both comments are sort of beside the point."

"Who's Katherine?" Eric and Kevin asked in unison.

"Katherine Witt," Alex replied with a smile, "is the director of practice growth at my firm. When Joe visited, he saw some of Katherine's work. I don't blame him for envying me having her."

"Does she have a clone?" Kevin joked.

"No"—Alex smiled—"but she doesn't really need one. You can get your own Katherine. The real question is *how*. In other words, here's the issue: Can Tiff be rehabilitated and developed professionally to the point where she gives you what you need in this regard? Or will you have to let her go too and try to fill both positions at the same time?"

Eric groaned, and Kevin rubbed his eyes. Both men then turned to Joe for his reaction. "I don't know," he said slowly. "Part of me wants to argue that of course she can do it, she can make the transition. But I have to wonder if any of that is wishful thinking on my part. After all, I hired her too."

After a protracted discussion, it developed that no one was enthusiastic about the prospect of dismissing Tiff and Ty simultaneously. Moreover, Eric believed Tiff could grow into the newly defined position, and Kevin was willing to give her the benefit of the doubt. He recommended, though, that she be put on a relatively short leash. "I reserve the right," he stressed, "to bring this up again if I still think she's out of her depth six months from now."

"Don't worry," Alex said in clipped tones. "If she's still out of her depth in six months, she'll be looking for a new job."

Then he made an extraordinary proposal. He offered to have Katherine take Tiff under her wing and act as a mentor to the young marketing director. Joe felt almost overwhelmed at his friend's generosity. He knew Katherine had a full slate of responsibilities at Weinstein & Federman and that the offer was a gracious and bountiful gift.

"Now comes the hard part," Alex said. "Harold."

"Yes, I noticed, back in there, how you shanghaied the discussion about him and cut it off," Kevin remarked.

"Just when it was getting good!" Charles put in, to a round of smiles.

"Well, the outlines of the situation, at least, were immediately apparent, and I thought it made sense to discuss the situation here instead of before the full partnership," Alex began. "The main sense I've gotten of

Harold so far is that he's counting the days till his retirement. What else can you tell me about him?"

Eric and Kevin looked at each other, then Kevin took a deep breath and plunged in. "I suppose I could tell you a million things, Alex, but what you just said is him in a nutshell—he's counting the days till he hangs it up."

"Tell him his nickname," Charles put in facetiously.

Kevin laughed mirthlessly. "The staff calls him Rip Van Winkle. RIP, you see, as an acronym for Retired in Place."

"Or Rest in Peace," Eric added.

"The firm fossil," Charles concluded.

"Every ten years, he wakes up and says or does something," Joe put in. "Then it's back to sleep for another however many years."

"You meant that, I know, as something of a joke," Alex said, "but that notion actually came through clearly in some of the staff questionnaire responses. The staff doesn't take him seriously, and there's a sense that the partners cover up for him to some extent." Alex dipped into his briefcase and pulled out some papers, then read a few responses, to the consternation of the C&P partners.

"He's a joke," one person had written. "But these partners stick together. I guess they're afraid it'll happen to them when they get old—that they'll end up like old Rip. What they don't realize is that people outside the firm hear the jokes too—even make 'em. I think it makes the whole firm look bad."

There was a long, long pause, and then Kevin broke the silence by returning to his favorite gripe. "And he's still drawing full compensation."

"That's serious enough," Eric acknowledged, "but there's more. Consider this: That's where you're going to find your real opposition to change—Harold. He's not going to agree to anything that doesn't pay off right here, right now, and certainly before he retires."

"Joe, do we know when that is, exactly?" Alex asked.

"He keeps changing the date." Joe sighed. "Last I heard, he was talking another year or two. And don't get the notion that it'll be easy to show him the door," he cautioned. "Harold's a tough nut to crack. He's been a partner almost from the very beginning. And when Old Man Potter hung it up seven years ago, it left him with the largest single block of stock. That means he has enough clout that nobody, including me, really wants to tangle with him."

"That's a part of leadership," Alex said simply. "But it sounds like what you all are telling me is that Harold is a detriment to this firm, that he doesn't pull his weight—that he's a hanger-on, in effect. Is that a fair assessment?"

"That sounds pretty harsh," Eric said.

"Look, none of this is personal," Alex explained. "It's a matter of survival for your firm. You said a few minutes ago that he was the biggest impediment to change. Heck, Joe couldn't even get him here for this meeting—despite the fact, as Kevin pointed out earlier, that Joe made it crystal clear how critical everyone's attendance was."

"That's right," Kevin weighed in, a look of dogged determination on his face. "Look, Alex is right. This isn't about Harold personally, or about anybody personally. If it was me standing in the way, I'd deserve to get knocked aside—unless I agreed to shape up."

"Do you think Harold will?" Alex asked. "Shape up?"

Four heads shook in unison. "Not a chance," Kevin said succinctly.

"He doesn't have it in him," Joe explained. "He thinks the rules don't apply to him, since he was practically a founding partner."

"We have a term for people like that," Alex said. The group waited expectantly. "Poison," he said quietly.

There was a lengthy pause, which Joe wanted to break but didn't. He felt in some way that if the group broke the wrong way on this issue, if they lacked the courage to take on Harold Brumlow, then there was little hope for Alex's broader plans. He felt as if he were balanced on tenterhooks while the other three men considered.

Finally Kevin broke the silence. "You're the expert," he said to Alex, "and I'm willing to follow your lead on this. It's not going to be pleasant, though, I'll tell you that."

Alex turned to the C&P managing partner. "Joe, we're at a point, I think, where you have to assume the lead."

"Right," Joe said, leaning forward, elbows on table. "Guys, this is an enormous step, one we have to weigh very, very carefully." The three other partners nodded. "There are also legal issues to consider. There's the partnership agreement, which gives Harold certain legal rights, and there'll be costs associated with this move. But before we get into that discussion, I want to ask everyone to take another moment or two to be absolutely certain about this. If anyone has a suggestion that they think might solve the problem without this drastic action, now's the time to bring it forward."

"Oh, let's at least kick it around some more," Eric said. He knew how much weight this decision carried; knew also that when the executive committee had to carry this news back to the partner group, each member would need to feel deeply certain that they'd given the matter the sober consideration it merited.

Charles sighed, with another pointed glance at his watch, but Kevin nodded emphatically. "You're right, Eric. Let's see if we can find another way through this—or around it—even if it isn't obvious."

So, as the minutes ticked away and the dinner hour approached and then passed, Charles fidgeted, while Kevin, Eric, and Joe wrestled with the problem of Harold. They considered every alternative they could conceive that fell short of forcing the elder partner out. They took a straw poll—just Xs, for anonymity, drawn next to the word "out" or "stays"—to see if anyone opposed the action but was reluctant to say so openly. No one was. They pumped Alex for suggestions. They took a break to give the matter individual thought. Their stomachs rumbled, but they ignored them and forged on.

Gradually, though, they ran dry, as it became increasingly clear that there *was* no alternative that wouldn't jeopardize the newly chosen direction. Joe waited until someone—Kevin—finally voiced the inevitable.

"I guess there's no other choice," Kevin said, and Eric nodded, both with grave faces. Charles, more nonchalant, merely shrugged his shoulders. "All right," Joe said heavily. "Then do I have a motion that this committee has decided to move Harold Brumlow into retirement?"

"I so move," Kevin said.

"Second," Eric said.

Charles affirmed, and Joe nodded at Alex. "It looks like that's it," he said.

"You'll need to do the research on this, Joe," Alex said. "I'll give you some pointers later on. One key issue is whether this is something the executive committee can act on unilaterally, or if it requires a vote of the full partnership.

"But for now"—he turned back to the small group—"you're agreed, and I congratulate you on being willing to tackle a truly tough issue.

"Now," he said, "there's only one more issue on the table, and this one may be the most important of all."

Wringing Hands

"Gentlemen," Alex said, "this is perhaps the most critical issue of all, and it centers around leadership. You all remember what we discussed earlier today, about Joe's abilities as a leader. That he's terrific at consensus building, but hasn't been able to implement an overall vision for Crandall & Potter.

"So the question, obviously, is how to put into place a framework that will allow that to happen. I'd like to start the conversation by inviting your comments. How do *you* think we can set that in motion?"

Joe smiled inwardly at Alex's finesse. He was too smart to just come out and tell them what to do.

There was silence for a few moments, as Kevin and Eric, if not Charles, appeared to be deep in thought. Finally Kevin spoke. "Well, one thing we need to do, obviously, is adopt more of what you called best practices—what Eric's been doing in health care. What was the whole phrase?"

"Product management best practices," Alex said. "And you're right, that's one key."

"We also talked a few minutes ago about taking steps to improve Tiff's effectiveness. That should help," Eric said.

"Absolutely," Alex said. "But part of it is in fact a leadership issue, isn't it? How would you tackle that aspect?"

"I would think there're probably two answers to that," Eric said slowly. "One might consist of Joe's updating his skills in this area, maybe getting a few pointers from you about being more assertive. We all agree that he spends far too much time managing personalities and keeping the peace—though we're the ones who've put him in that position. The other part would probably relate to how we support him in his efforts to lead. Just this moment, though, beyond the obvious— letting go of some of the petty stuff we saddle him with, the nonsense that keeps him *busy* keeping the peace—I don't know what that would look like."

"You're right on both counts, Eric," Alex said. "Joe is going to get a crash course over the next few months, to learn how to lead a dynamically growing firm. That's something I've helped many MPs learn. But you're also right that without the full, active support of the partners, that effort will go nowhere. And here's where we get to the nitty gritty that affects you as partners.

"The partners need to make a commitment to allow Joe to lead this firm on a full-time basis. At the end of our discussion this afternoon, the partner group as a whole decided on a goal of 15-percent growth. That's a terrific goal, and very realistic if you put the pieces in place.

"To do that, you'll need to do two things, the same two things my firm did. First, identify leaders for each segment of firm revenue and create an incentive component for their compensation, a component that's tied to their segment's performance."

Alex paused for effect. "Second, bite the bullet and make a commitment to compensate your managing partner on a full-time basis, and let him drop his book of business."

Whew, Joe thought. *It's out there on the table, at long last. And now the fireworks start.*

"Well, I don't know that dropping his book of business is a problem," Charles observed. "I think a lot of the guys would love to divvy that up."

"I'm not sure you heard everything he just said," Kevin pointed out. "He also said, 'Pay Joe full time for being MP. *Just* for being MP.'"

"That would be a problem," Charles said.

"Not so fast," Eric cut in. "Let's hear him out."

"It's brutally simple, guys," Alex said. "You need a full-time leader, and you need to back that up with bucks. Joe has to make a real commitment for this to succeed, and that won't happen if he has to be looking over his shoulder the whole time. It won't work."

"Sketch it out for us a little more," Eric requested.

"Okay. Let me tell you a little about what happened at my firm. Weinstein & Federman was founded by my father, probably about the same time Crandall & Potter was getting its start. And it went along, probably a lot like C&P, doing okay but no great shakes, everybody fairly content and nobody making waves. When my father died, about eighteen years ago, I took the helm.

"I knew I needed to make real changes, because I saw how much the business climate was changing. And I was able to pull it off. But I won't lie to you; it took a lot of blood, sweat, and tears. What's more, I had a real advantage over Joe, because my dad founded the firm.

"But I'll tell you exactly what I told Joe a few weeks ago: When I started out, my partner group was just like yours. There was no sense of common purpose, and people didn't talk to each other. So nobody knew what anybody else was working on, just like you. Also just like you, we lost a lot of business that way.

"Nobody—inside or outside the firm—knew what our specialties were, so we chased every lead we heard about, like a dog that chases every car that goes down the street. You're right, Kevin, you act that way and one day you wake up and realize that even you, the partners, don't know what your client profile is.

"We also didn't know how to pursue leads effectively, so, like the dog I just mentioned, most of the time we'd end up, when the chase was over, emptyhanded and with our tongues hanging out.

"Oh, we had one more fatal flaw in common with you, too. We had great technicians but no real segment leaders.

"That, guys, is the crux of the problem. To achieve real, lasting growth, you *must* have leaders for each segment and a managing partner running the show."

"What would that look like, in black-and-white terms?" Eric asked.

"Here's what it looks like at Weinstein & Federman. I manage the firm, and it's my full-time job, ten hours a day, five days a week. My job is simple. I'm in charge of the firm and the vision—which translates to, the partners and the way they *execute* the plan. At this point, years into the effort, it's pretty much a finely tuned engine, but it still needs adjustments from time to time. It's my job to provide those adjustments and keep the engine humming."

Noting a quizzical look on Eric's face, Alex realized he needed to be more specific. "Let me give you an example. At Weinstein, we have a method we call 'divide and conquer.' Here's what it means: When you're developing an opportunity, you have to figure out who the decision makers are at the target company and assign individuals from your firm to develop relationships with each of them. It has to be done one on one. It's a highly effective strategy, but it never comes about naturally. Somebody has to set it up and reinforce it constantly. From now on, that'll be Joe's job.

"The MP also makes the tough calls and eliminates turf battles. When a new lead comes in, the MP decides who'll head up the effort to land it, and that decision has nothing to do with who brought it in the door—or, even worse, who happened to pick up the phone when the call came in from the prospect.

"He'll make those assignments based on who's best suited to pursue the lead, taking into account things like fit between partner and prospect and relationship skills certain partners possess. He'll also ride herd on the pack, to make sure the 'my client' way of thinking doesn't creep back in. At the new Crandall & Potter, the clients will belong to the firm, not to any particular partner. Joe will make that happen. In other words, he'll be in charge of the team.

"He'll be your manager—for the first time ever, really."

Eric nodded, but Alex decided to dangle one more idea before them. "Let me give you just one more concrete example. From time to time, every firm hits certain points where, in order to get to the next level in terms of growth, you need to make changes in your approach, become more sophisticated in your techniques. Again, that's the MP's job—in fact, there's no one else who *can* do that job, because there's nobody else who's paid to look into the future, to look at the big picture."

Now Kevin was beginning to nod too, but cautiously. "And you can pretty much guarantee that this approach will bring us up to the kind of growth other firms are seeing?"

"Well, what in life is guaranteed? But I *can* tell you this with absolute confidence: If the partners commit to this course and stick with it, you'll get results. You're going to have to work hard, though, and learn new ways of doing your jobs."

"So that's all we have to do," Kevin said. "We agree to work hard, we hand over the reins to Joe, give him carte blanche to do this full time, pay him to do nothing else, and then . . . what do we do, send away for a kit? *CPA Practice Growth in Five Easy Steps*? I can't believe it's that easy."

Alex grinned, shaking his head. "Of course it's not. I didn't mean to oversimplify. Look, here's how it works. A firm like yours decides it wants to grow. Typically you go out and find someone who understands the Practice Growth Model. This could be a leader from another firm, someone from your CPA association, or it could be a consultant.

"This person basically becomes your firm's mentor. The person comes in, meets the partners, gets a real feel for what you're doing, sits in on meetings, then goes away and puts together an approach tailored to your firm. Then they check back in from time to time—to troubleshoot problems that come up during the transition, to make sure you stay on the right track, to evaluate the results you're getting. And when the MP finds himself in water over his head—and it always happens, believe me—this person is there to lead you safely through to the other side. This is definitely *not* do-it-yourself work."

Alex smiled. "But you guys got lucky. Joe and I met and hit it off, and it happens that I've been through this a number of times—doing basically what the consultants do when they come in. I've spent a lot of time talking with Joe about your firm, and now I've met the partners, spent some time with you all, so I have a very good feel for your operation.

"I can do what the consultant would—guide Joe and mentor him as he implements the Practice Growth Model in your firm."

"For what fee?" Charles asked pointedly.

Alex smiled equably. "I do a few of these from time to time, and I don't charge for it. I kind of look on it as pro bono work."

"Will you be onsite a lot, checking in on how we're doing?" Eric asked.

"I'll come visit from time to time, yes," Alex said. "But I'll be in close touch with Joe on a continuing basis, and he'll act as my eyes and ears. If something comes up that he hasn't encountered before, he'll get in touch with me, and we'll figure it out together.

"It's really mostly a matter of experience," Alex finished. "There's no one-size-fits-all approach because there are too many variables, and each situation is unique in some ways. It's the ability to provide overarching guidance that I bring to the table. Joe will be responsible for all the day-to-day implementation and leadership."

"So you're saving us a big chunk of green, huh, Alex?" Charles asked disingenuously.

"Well, I'll say this," he replied mildly. "You'll be getting my services for free, but I've been around plenty of firms that paid consultants to do this work. I've yet to hear anybody complain afterward, about the results or the cost. This is an approach that works."

"What kind of growth is your firm seeing, Alex?" Kevin asked, eager to get back to the point.

"Twenty percent per year, sustained," Alex answered succinctly.

"Wow," Kevin said, as Eric mouthed the same word silently.

It All Rests with Joe

"Understand that you won't get there overnight," Alex cautioned.

"What kind of time frame would you envision?" Eric asked.

"Two to three years altogether."

"Two to three years!" Kevin exclaimed. "My heavens and earth!"

"Whoa, now, take it easy; let me explain," Alex said soothingly. "This is a process that will play out over time. You'll be making changes, and seeing results, all along. So it may be two or three years before you fit the last few pieces into the puzzle, but at every step of the way, you'll be making changes that'll improve your effectiveness.

"In the first year, for instance, you'll develop your strategic growth plan, train your people to carry it out, and start to put it in place. So at the end of year one, you'll already have something new and solid to stand on.

"Then you spend the next two years refining your implementation, applying the knowledge and experience you gain as you go along. So you probably won't realize the whole panoply of benefits for two or three years, but you'll definitely see improvement within a year or so." Alex paused to assess Kevin's reaction. He was pleased to see the tax partner nod.

"That makes sense," Kevin mused.

"There's one more thing that might not have occurred to you," Alex went on. "As I said, I've been doing this for some time—coaching firms that want to make the transition to growth—and not every MP is willing to take on the challenge. This is a huge risk for Joe, and he has to trust you partners implicitly to keep up your end of the bargain. Becoming a full-time MP, and learning everything he'll have to know, will involve an enormous amount of work for him. If he weren't up to the challenge, you'd be facing a very different kind of decision: whether to settle for anemic growth or look for a new MP. I've seen firms struggle with that particular conundrum, and it's not a pretty sight."

"All right, then, let's talk dollars and cents," Kevin said. "What's this going to cost us?"

"This is what it amounts to," Alex said. "You need to commit to letting Joe give up his book of business during a transition period. He'll become full-time managing partner, and you'll provide written assurance that you won't change your minds after a year or two. Here's why: Every MP looking at making this change has a fear deep down that they'll give up their book of business, take on this new responsibility, then after a year or so the partners will run out of patience and decide things weren't all that bad the old way.

"But of course there's no going back at that point—for the MP, at least. So he needs assurance that you guys are serious, that you won't cut and run. By the way, that extends to his retirement plan as well. He has to know that his retirement compensation won't suffer because he made this change."

At these words, Kevin winced audibly, and Charles was emboldened to speak. "Well, I must say that as far as I'm concerned personally, I consider this out of the question. We are not going to pay Joe to be a full-time cheerleader while the rest of us do all the work."

"You may have missed what I said a minute ago, Charles," Alex replied evenly. "Believe me, Joe's going to be working harder than any of you."

"All right, then," Charles replied. "Strike the part about the work. I will say simply that we aren't going to make him the kind of financial guarantees you've described."

"Now hold on a second," Kevin put in. "You started out by saying you were speaking for yourself, Charles, and I think you'd better keep it that way. We're here to discuss this issue, not listen to you decide it for us."

"Kevin, please," Charles said. "You heard what he said. It's a bunch of touchy-feely mumbo jumbo, straight out of Mary Poppins. Sounds more like full-time cheerleader and nanny to me."

"Maybe so, but it seems to be working for a lot of other firms," Eric put in. He spread his hands. "Look, it makes no sense to refuse to change with the times, Charles. We know the old way isn't working."

"The money does concern me a bit," Kevin admitted. "Can you be any more specific about how these changes will affect earnings?"

"They'll grow modestly for the next couple of years," Alex said candidly. "Then you'll start to see the payback."

"I just don't know . . . " Kevin's voice trailed off uncertainly.

"Look, Kevin," Alex said. "The firm's slow growth rate has been a real sore spot for you lately, right? Well, guess what? There's no magic pill you can take. There's a real-world solution, and this is it. So in a sense, it's either put up or shut up. I hate to be so blunt, but that's the bottom line.

"I'll tell you one more thing, too. Either get onboard wholeheartedly, or don't do it at all. For this transition to be successful, we need the buy-in of those guys out there—the partners. You three are the ones who'll have to sell this to them, not me. I can explain it and relate what I've seen, but the partners will be looking to you three for direction."

Kevin and Eric looked at each other, then lapsed into silence. At length, Kevin spoke. "I hope this isn't out of line, but I have a request." He turned to face his firm's MP. "Joe, I'd like us to have a few words alone with Alex, if you don't mind."

Joe reddened slightly, but rose after only a moment's hesitation. "No problem, Kevin. Should I give you—about how long, do you think?"

"Ten minutes ought to do it."

After Joe had stepped from the room, Kevin spoke. "Alex, I think I'm about ready to take the plunge on this thing. You were right, I've been frustrated for a long time by our results, and if this is the solution, I'm all for it. But I want your personal opinion—and I hope you'll be brutally honest—on one thing."

Kevin took a deep breath. "I've known Joe for years, and he's a good man. What's more, he's a good friend. What I *don't* know is whether he's the right guy for this. He's pretty easygoing, you know? And he's never done anything like this before. It looks like he's become a friend of yours too, but I'm asking you for the truth anyway: Do you think he's got it in him to take this on? To make it work?"

Alex leaned back and interlaced his fingers behind his head. "I *will* be honest, Kevin. Joe and I first talked about growth back in June, at an industry meeting in Chicago. I sensed then a real interest in growth on his part, but there was also a deep-seated reluctance I couldn't place. I've learned since what was going on in his head. He'd heard about new tactics and approaches in the field, but he was all but convinced his partners wouldn't go for it. Hey, I know for a fact that he tried to get C&P involved in one new area, 404, and was told by one of the partners point blank that it was the wrong kind of work for this firm to pursue."

Charles felt his face start to burn and was consumed with hope that the others wouldn't notice. He remembered that conversation with Joe. He had pointed out that the firm didn't have the resources or the people to get into that new area. Well, they didn't. Was it his, Charles's, fault that other, forward-looking firms had developed those resources? *Ah, what the heck,* he decided. *Let 'em do whatever they want.*

Alex had kept his eyes trained on Kevin as he spoke, but he'd still noted the play of emotions on Charles's face. *If it serves to shut him up, fine,* he thought. "So the short answer is, yes, I think Joe has what it takes. I know he feels keenly the responsibility for this firm that Al Potter entrusted to him. He's grown more laid back over the years, I'm sure, but in candidness, I believe that's what you partners have wanted. Can you honestly say you wanted a real leader before?

"I think he'll step up, though; if I didn't think so, I wouldn't be here." Alex leaned forward in his chair abruptly. "I don't waste my time, or my practice growth director's, and I'm preparing to make a significant investment of both in your firm."

"I don't suppose we can do this on a trial basis," Kevin said reluctantly.

"Absolutely not."

"All right, then," Kevin declared. "I'm in. In for good."

"Same here," Eric said.

Three sets of eyes turned to Charles, who yawned ostentatiously. "Who am I to stand in the way of progress?" he said sweetly.

"Terrific," Alex said. "Eric, could you see if Joe's outside and grab him?"

When everyone was seated again, Alex said, "The executive committee has come to a unanimous decision to throw its full support behind this effort. Tomorrow morning, when the partners reconvene, the real push will start."

The Practice Growth Model

"This is the part I always look forward to," Alex said by way of opening the next morning's meeting. "We spent all day yesterday talking about the problem, but today we get to focus on the solution."

Alex rubbed his hands together, fairly radiating enthusiasm. "Last night during the executive committee meeting, Kevin asked me how much growth my firm, Weinstein & Federman, has experienced. The answer is twenty percent per year, and that's sustained growth."

"Yeah, but you've probably had lots of mergers," Frank observed sardonically. "That always helps."

"We haven't had one," Alex said, then paused to let that information sink in. "We do it by using a specific model, one I'm going to tell you about now.

"It's called the Practice Growth Model, and it has two distinct parts. The first part is a specific rainmaking process with four steps. The second part is the practice growth levers—four disciplines we use to manage the rainmaking process.

"If that sounds a bit confusing, take my word, it isn't. But, come to think of it, *don't* take my word for it. Let me just sketch it out for you, and you'll see for yourselves."

Alex turned and lifted the cover sheet from his flipchart, revealing four boxes in a row.

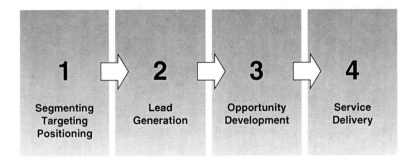

"This is the rainmaking process," he said. "All effective rainmaking incorporates these four steps; if any of them is missing, you can't juice the growth engine. In step one, we segment and target our markets and position the firm properly in each segment. If step one is done correctly, then step two, lead generation, follows logically, almost automatically. If step two is carried out properly, we then have opportunities, which we develop in step three. And, finally, if we develop our opportunities properly, we land clients and deliver services—step four.

"I know this looks pretty simple, but is everybody with me so far?" Alex looked out to see mostly nods and only a few yawns. He nodded. "At our firm, it took us a while to realize that each of these activities is different, requiring different people, different training, different methodologies. We thought of business development as just one big, amorphous hodgepodge of pursuing and winning business. We had no idea it needed to be so specific!

"And we weren't the only ones. There's a critical error that nearly all CPAs make: They don't distinguish between step two, lead generation, and step three, opportunity development. We didn't either, until we learned how.

"But once we started to get our arms around the process, we could see that each part of it needs to be managed differently. This is where the Practice Growth Model part of the equation comes in. As I said, it has four 'levers'—tools we use to manage the rainmaking process, and consequently the growth of our firm."

At this point, Alex knew the partners would be shifting in their seats, starting to lose the thread of the explanation. He turned to deliver some encouragement. "It'll start to make sense once you see it sketched out. And this part, at least, will look a little familiar to you, since we talked about these tools yesterday."

He turned back to his flipchart and underneath the existing four boxes, he filled in four more.

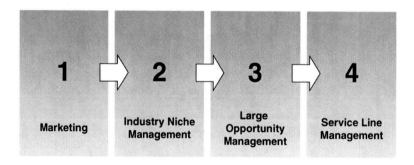

"Now, these are the four levers we use to manage growth—the practice growth levers. We saw them first yesterday, but we didn't have a name for them then. Now we do.

"Just as with the rainmaking steps, everybody uses these four levers, whether they realize it or not. But few people use them *well*. Yesterday we devoted a good deal of time to talking about how Crandall & Potter has used these levers. We talked about your approach to marketing—which has been a tactical toolbox and nothing more. There's no vision or coordination in your marketing efforts. You pick up awards here and there, but the whole effort is disjointed.

"Next we have industry niche management, which we decided is also haphazard. Why? Because we've never encouraged leadership; we've simply let the partner who seemed most interested in an industry work it. There *has* been the occasional success. Eric has made great strides in developing his niche, but, tellingly, no one else has the slightest idea how he did it.

"Next we come to large opportunity management, and you know what a huge problem this has been for your firm, both in terms of personnel and the way partners have worked at cross purposes with each other. Finally, service line management, where we've simply appointed the best technicians as service line leaders. But they focus only on stage four of the rainmaking process, service delivery, so very little thought is given to the growth of the service lines.

"Well," Alex said, "that's where you are, but where could you be? Where might you like to be?"

Alex walked away from the flipchart and began strolling around the room, hands in his pants pockets, speaking casually and making eye contact with individual partners as he spoke. "Can you envision a marketing effort in which all activities are *specifically* focused on growth? Where the sales and marketing work is interconnected? Where the marketing director works closely and effectively with partners, and where marketing efforts translate seamlessly into lead generation? How about a system where the marketing director works only on projects that will *enhance revenue* and always asks about this before anything new is launched? That's what your marketing effort can look like one year from now."

Alex continued moving about the room, addressing the partners one by one and gaining thoughtful nods in return. "Industry niche management. Each segment will have a leader, and the *incentive* portion of the leader's compensation will be tied to performance." Alex saw several partners react visibly and decided to stem the tide of anxiety. "Understand, this is a terrific opportunity for these segment leaders, because they will in effect begin to control their own earnings. You'll have partners in place who'll turn their segments into dynamos once they learn how—and we're going to teach them how."

Alex had made his way about halfway around the room by this time. "You'll have a more effective business developer and a strong working relationship between the marketing and business development heads— who, by the way, will also be paid based on their production. Your segment leaders will gain high-quality leads through the stronger ties they'll develop with their respective associations—just as Eric has already done, to such marvelous effect." Eric nodded in appreciation of the compliment.

"You'll all be 'researching the ecosystem,' which simply means that you'll be meeting with people in your industry who can help you define your strategic direction and lead you to likely buyers. One by one, the segments will start to take shape, and your pipeline will mushroom with leads. They'll be high-percentage prospects, too, not the catch-as-catch-can leads of the past. Perhaps most important, everyone at Crandall & Potter will know exactly where they fit into the picture; they'll know just what part of the program they're responsible for carrying out.

"Questions so far?" Alex asked.

"No, go on," Durwood said after a slight pause. "This is intriguing."

"Yes," Alex said. "Also very exciting, once you get into it.

"Large opportunity management," he went on, and here he saw several partners wince. "Before long, you'll be smiling, not cringing," Alex promised. "Within two months, your pipeline could just about double. Within eight to nine months, your win rate may go from forty-five percent, where it is now, to sixty-five percent. By year two, you could have twenty percent of annual revenue in your pipeline at any point in time, and, as Joe told you several weeks ago, that's where it needs to be.

"You partners won't be wasting time anymore on proposals you have no hope of closing. What's more, you'll be talking with each other, and you'll be amazed how good that feels! Every new opportunity will be visible to everyone immediately, so you won't lose out anymore because your right hand didn't know what your left hand was doing.

"If *anyone* in the firm has an inside track with a prospect, the partner in charge of the prospect will hear about it right away. Your pipeline will be a window into your future staffing needs. You'll be able to hire the right technical talent based on anticipated demand.

"The marketing director and business developer will be on the same page, working hand in glove. And for the first time ever, perhaps, you'll find yourselves competing with larger firms—and winning!

"Last but assuredly not least, let's look ahead to service line management, which will make its long-awaited debut at Crandall & Potter. You'll no longer miss out on market opportunities for new services. Your firm's portfolio will become more balanced. You'll find yourself competing less on price and more on value. You'll be innovative, be able to differentiate your services, and your firm will be positioned effectively with various buyer groups. You'll be using what we call a 'dashboard' to keep track of targets and performance in industries, service lines, and large opportunities."

Alex had reached the front of the room by now, and he turned to face the group confidently. "Your firm, in a word, will be transformed. And it will happen, not by magic, but simply by adhering to the Practice Growth Model—the template I used to turn my firm around, one I've helped many firms just like yours put in place."

Alex paused. "I've spent the most of the morning telling you what the future can look like. Let's take a short break now, and when we come back, we'll get cracking on the nuts and bolts."

The Practice Growth Model in Action

After the break, the group reconvened, fortified with coffee and seemingly eager to tackle the discussion Alex had promised.

"I'm going to start with a brief review," he said once everyone was seated. "Yesterday, in addition to talking about the problems we've had in the past, we talked about developing a three-year growth plan that will bring us, by the end of that period, to growth on the order of 16 percent." Heads nodded in agreement, and Alex went on.

"We also talked about the lack of a common vision, and we agreed that once we develop one, it'll be up to the managing partner to keep us on track to achieve it. Right?" More nods. "So, as we go on from here, let's try to keep our conversation focused on those things."

At this point, Alex invited discussion, and most of the partners plunged in eagerly. Fairly early, it was apparent that there was some confusion about the interplay between the rainmaking process and practice growth levers, so Alex drew a diagram of the whole process on the flipchart.

The Practice Growth Model

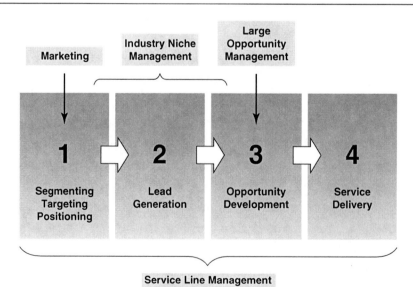

"Walk through it with me," Alex said. "You use the marketing lever to manage your firm's segmenting/targeting/positioning efforts. The

large opportunity management lever controls the opportunity development part of rainmaking. The industry niche management lever is mostly about lead generation, but begins with segmenting/targeting/positioning, and helps with opportunity development. Finally, the service line management lever focuses on all four stages, as service line leaders decide how to bring services to market successfully, launch innovations in current offerings, and ensure that service delivery is efficient.

"What it really boils down to is that nothing is random anymore—nothing. Every step of the way, as you develop and pursue leads, there's a process and a key individual in place to keep tabs on what's going on, and to bring it back into line if it strays. And though it may look unwieldy when I draw it up here on the board, once the system's been in place for a few months, it will feel as natural as rolling out of bed in the morning. It will be the foundation of everything you do, and you'll wonder how you ever got along without it."

"I don't know about this," Frank's nasal tones rang out. "I'm starting to think Charles was on to something yesterday, when he called it mumbo jumbo."

"It's anything but," Alex said crisply, "so let me give you some examples." He turned to Joe. "What are your firm's average billable hours per partner?"

"About twelve-fifty," Joe replied.

"Okay. What happens to those other six hundred fifty hours?" Before Joe could answer, Alex turned to address the whole group. "Not just Joe on this one—somebody else?"

After a brief period of uncomfortable silence, Alex chuckled reassuringly. "This is not a test, I promise you!"

Amid general laughter, Ben spoke up. "Well, with the exception of Kevin, I imagine we all spend a fair amount of time sitting at our desks eating lunch. Or we're out on sales calls, meeting with prospects. Maybe Ty gave us a lead; maybe another partner asked us to come along on one of their calls."

"And what do you get out of that?" Alex asked.

"Generally, not much," Ben replied honestly.

"Right," Alex said. "Because if you're not working within this Model, all the networking in the world goes for naught, because it's entirely random, and random efforts don't get results." Alex paused for breath and went on.

"Let's take another practice growth lever, and another rainmaking step. The first step in successful rainmaking is segmenting/targeting/positioning, or STP. STP is often laid at the doorstep of the marketing director. But not in our Model. It's simple. Partners know their clients and markets best, so they're the ones who need to be doing STP, with the marketing director providing guidance.

"But is that the way it happens at C&P? No! Because the partners for the most part ignore the marketing director, and then she ignores you right back, mapping out her own programs and going her own way. So the STP process is chaotic, and the marketing effort goes nowhere."

"All right, let's say we buy in to the Model, theoretically at least," Smith said. "Show us how it changes the way things actually play out."

"Okay," Alex said. "Instead of essentially wasting a big chunk of those six hundred fifty hours a year, you'll start spending them 'researching the ecosystem.' As I said before, that means, essentially, determining where your best opportunities lie, so you can exploit them most effectively.

"Whoa!" Smith said. "I want to do my part, for sure, but I don't think I have an extra six hundred fifty hours to spend on research, no matter what Joe says!"

After the laughter died down, Alex went on. "You'll find out how much time you have once we get into it, Smith. But the crux of the matter is this: The partners are crucial to the industry niche management and service line management levers, and you 'hook into' the marketing and large opportunity management levers as well. The bottom line? You can't just delegate marketing and selling to staff. You have to do it yourselves, and you have to do it right!

"So let's take a minute to look at the numbers. Let's say a three-hundred-dollar-per-hour partner can work heads down for twenty hours, over whatever period of time, and bill six thousand dollars' worth of business. That partner could spend the same twenty hours working within the efficient Practice Growth Model system of generating and developing business and produce revenue at *ten times* six thousand dollars.

"This is about leverage.

"It's a matter of efficiency—of being a finely tuned engine versus Chitty Chitty Bang Bang."

As the discussion moved forward, Alex continued to provide the broad outlines of the discussion, while the partners brought up specific situations and asked how the Practice Growth Model would apply. Gradually, most of them began to catch on, and every once in a while the room would ring with excitement, as another connection was made.

"I think I'm actually starting to get it," Kevin said later. "We have the four levers, and we use them to manage—to maximize, really—our growth efforts. Is that a fair statement, Alex?"

"It is," Alex replied.

"So it's really as basic as debits left, credits right," Kevin said. "Levers and growth. Four levers, and the levers manage growth."

"You got it."

"I think this makes sense, everybody," Kevin said, looking around at his fellow partners. "Alex, could we break for lunch now? I think we need some time to let all this sink in and maybe to talk to each other a little."

"Good suggestion," Alex said, and they adjourned for their midday repast.

"We're in the home stretch now," Alex said as the group reconvened after eating. "This is crunch time—time to make some decisions. I was able to listen in on some of your conversations during the lunch break. I'd like us to bring those discussions in here, if we can. We need to get everything— your enthusiasms and your concerns—out on the table, so we can talk about them."

After some initial reluctance, partners began to speak up. Some were chary of committing to such a major program of change. Others thought they were willing, but needed some idea of the scope of the new approach, both in time and dollars. Once launched on the new program, was the firm committed for all time, or could they reverse course later if they chose?

All afternoon, the partners kicked the issue around. Alex was grateful for each new question, because nearly every one gave him another opportunity to delve a little more deeply into how the Practice Growth Model works. It was gratifying to see the faces of the partners clear one by one, as the confusion started to lift. One partner after another came to grasp how the Model would let them address problems that, in some cases, had been festering for years.

Not everyone came along on this voyage of discovery, of course. Charles, who sat stone faced through the entire day, finally announced disdainfully that he had "no interest whatsoever in 'exploring the ecosystem'—whatever that may turn out to be."

And Frank continued to quibble with everyone, on both sides of every issue.

But little by little, the partners seemed to edge their way toward endorsing the plan. "Finally, we're getting everybody on the same page!" Kevin declared with obvious satisfaction at one point.

By late afternoon, it seemed that a consensus was building, and finally Alex moved to bring the meeting to a close. "I think we're about there," he summarized. "What I'm hearing seems to be overall agreement that the Model sounds good. But a lot of you would like to see what it looks like in action, and so I'd like to extend an invitation. If you'll choose two or three partners, I'd love to have them join me at my firm for a few days. They can sit in on meetings, talk with my partners and my staff, and ask whatever they want. How does that sound?"

Heads bobbed in enthusiastic acceptance of Alex's proposal, and Kevin, Eric, and Matthew were quickly appointed as the delegation. As Alex turned the meeting back over to Joe for closing, both noted an air of resolve that was almost palpable in the room. *They're coming together,* Alex thought. *They're well on their way now to becoming a team.*

PART III

BUSINESS DISCIPLINE BRINGS PRACTICE GROWTH

Dawn of a New Day

Three weeks later, Kevin, Eric, and Matthew stepped off a plane at the Minneapolis-St. Paul airport, chock-full of enthusiasm and eager to get back to the office to start spreading the news. What an eye-opener these past four days had been! The Crandall & Potter partners had roamed completely at will throughout Alex's firm, pumping his partners for information: first for some history about their firm before Alex's growth initiative, then for personal experiences and opinions about the transition, and finally for details of the amazing operation they were witnessing.

On their last day there, Alex had Katherine sit down with Kevin and Eric, as representatives of the C&P executive committee, and examine the compensation plan for Weinstein & Federman partners. They didn't merely glance at the plan; they pored over it, devouring the details of tracking opportunities, clients, and productivity.

It was very close to what Joe had experienced when he'd visited back in early October. The partners came away with the same strong conclusion he had drawn: that this was a firm, and an approach, they should emulate. Kevin in particular could hardly believe the strong, effective alliance that existed between partners and other leaders at Weinstein & Federman. The director of practice growth, Katherine Witt, ran a tight ship. As Kevin told Eric the first evening, nearly breathless with hope, "If she can teach Tiff even a third of what she knows, our firm'll never be the same!"

Matthew was most impressed with the deep commonality of purpose among the W&F partners. There was no bickering about clients, no undercutting of others' efforts, and—most unbelievable to Matthew—no scorekeeping as to who had brought in what business. He was a bit reluctant to express all this quite so bluntly to the more senior partners, but then Eric himself made the same point. "These partners don't compete with one another; they're all playing on the same team, with *no evidence of egos.* Amazing!"

They made notes furiously, lapping up a new argot, jotting down reminders to ask Alex about this, or follow up with Katherine about that. "We're such abecedarians here," Eric told Kevin and Matthew. "Almost nothing we've known so far in our careers—about how to work together, how to pursue prospects—applies anymore."

"I've noticed, when I talk to Katherine," Matthew observed, "that she talks a lot about discipline. Disciplined direction, disciplined approach to selecting which leads to pursue, disciplined efforts to developing the leads."

"Opportunities," Kevin corrected. "They call them opportunities."

"It's like a brave new world," Eric said, shaking his head. "I had no idea . . . and there's so much to learn."

"Oh, we'll learn," Kevin promised. "Just watch us learn."

The next few months saw some uncomfortable moments unfold at Crandall & Potter. As soon as Joe returned from the strategic summit, he bit the bullet and met with Ty, dismissing him, to the younger man's enormous consternation. "The Ty-Guy gets it!" he kept insisting, though he'd barely let Joe get a word out once he'd realized where the agenda lay. "The Ty-Guy can turn it around for you! You've gotta give me one more chance!"

Joe could tell he was wavering, then checked himself with a start. He was the leader here! He had a responsibility to this firm. He quietly but firmly told Ty that the decision was final, then negotiated a quick but fair settlement that had Ty out of the building and on his way quietly and without incident. Notification of partners and staff could then take place in a low-key manner that left few ruffled feathers.

He began poring over the materials Alex sent him to study and making a list of major issues to be addressed. He took a careful look at the partnership agreement and met with the firm's attorney to discuss the early retirement planned for Harold.

He also began drawing up his final list of major market segments and service lines for Crandall & Potter, along with proposed leaders for the segments. In some cases, such as Eric in health care and Kevin in tax, the choice was clear. In others, as with Charles in audit, it was less so. Charles had unambiguously turned down the responsibility previously, yet he was far and away the senior audit partner. So what to do? On Alex's advice, Joe began putting out feelers for a new partner, one who could match Charles's technical heft in audit but who had equivalent experience implementing the Practice Growth Model.

Once Ty was gone, Joe began preparing the partners for the fact that they'd eventually need a new business developer. Some were reluctant, having been burned so badly by Ty that they never wanted to see that seat occupied again. Joe began the process of educating them about why the job was important, telling them again how crucial the position was to the second and third levers (industry niche management and large opportunity management) of the Practice Growth Model.

He began drafting the incentive compensation component of an overall compensation plan for both segment leaders and key staff (business developer and marketing director)—one that would tie their compensation directly to performance. He mapped out a preliminary proposal for his own compensation and retirement plan, a task he found more challenging than he'd expected. He ultimately decided to adopt the model Weinstein & Federman had used for Alex, one that guaranteed a certain base pay for four years and added an incentive package based on overall growth and profitability within the firm.

He made preparations to give up his book of business. He delivered pep talks to partners as they continued to talk among themselves—sometimes hopefully, sometimes nervously—about the future direction the firm would take.

And, finally, on the morning the three partners were preparing to leave for Philadelphia, Joe had a heart-to-heart talk with Tiff.

"I'm so excited," Tiff enthused as she took a seat in Joe's office. "Everything we've been talking about since the summit. It's too much! I just can't wait to get started!"

Joe could sense the undercurrent of nervousness. He'd met with Tiff briefly after Ty's ouster, both to let her know, tacitly, that she was not set to follow him out the door, and to tell her they'd be getting together soon for an in-depth look at how her job would change over the coming months.

Still, he could tell Tiff was tense about the changed environment at Crandall & Potter. "I want to start, Tiff, by filling you in some more about the summit," he began. "I want you to feel free to ask questions as I go along. It's crucial that you understand this new model for growth we're adopting, the Practice Growth Model."

For nearly an hour, Joe described the events of the weekend meeting, culminating with a detailed explanation of how the four-stage rain-making process fit into the Practice Growth Model. "This is where we're going, Tiff," he said, "and you're an important player from here on."

"I'm really pleased to hear it. To be honest, Joe, I've never felt the partners truly needed or appreciated me," Tiff confided.

Joe nodded, but frowned. "That may be," he said, "but we have to stop resurrecting the past. From now on, we move forward with a clean slate."

At this point, Tiff smiled and unveiled her latest effort—a collaboration with an advertising agency on a new logo for the brochure she'd been developing. "This is a great case in point," Joe said. "Here's the first question you need to ask yourself: 'Is this going to increase revenue? If it is, how?'"

"Well," Tiff said uncertainly, "I guess it'll increase sales." She paused, hesitating. "The brochure, you mean," she added.

"Yes, the brochure. In what way will it increase revenue?"

"Well, gosh, Joe, everybody needs a nice brochure . . . " Tiff's voice trailed off, and she bit her lip, perplexed. "I guess I don't really understand. How could a brochure increase revenue?"

"Exactly!" Joe said, nodding emphatically. "A new brochure, by itself, won't—that's the point. So you get together with the partners, and you work with *them*—not the ad agency. And you find out whether they—the partners—understand what we're trying to do; you work with them to figure out why we even need a new brochure. Make sure *they* can answer the hard questions. Such as: Are we trying to create awareness in a market? If so, which market? Why?

"Tiff, from now on, we're going to be much more hard-nosed about how we spend money to create awareness."

Tiff shook her head slowly in reluctant disagreement. "But that's not how it's done, Joe."

"It is here," Joe said firmly. "From here on out, every decision, every activity you undertake, is done *exactly* that way."

It was clear that Tiff was nonplussed, but Joe pressed ahead, remembering the strategy Alex had suggested. "You have to start changing the way you look at your job, Tiff," he said, "and you have to understand that it isn't optional. From now on, you have one job: support and provide resources for the partners. Strengthen their effectiveness in generating leads and pursuing opportunities."

Joe slapped his desk. "Don't develop any more brochures until you and the partners together have a solid understanding of what the market needs. And *help them gain this understanding.*"

Joe paused to give his next words added import. "Your own effectiveness—and, ultimately, your future here—depend on this. Do you understand?"

Tiff nodded but retained a look of misery. Joe went on in a milder tone. "Fortunately, you won't have to go it alone." He told Tiff of Alex's offer to have Katherine Witt act as mentor to her. Tiff's relief was apparent, and she left his office noticeably less forlorn than she'd seemed minutes earlier, on her way to put in a call to Katherine.

"I'm counting on you, Tiff," Joe said as she was preparing to leave. "Don't let me down. Don't let yourself down."

"I won't," she said. As she closed the door behind her, Joe briefly considered the odds on her success. No better than 50-50, he decided fatalistically. He shrugged and turned back to his work.

Welcome!

The final shift in momentum came when Kevin, Eric, and Matthew began relating what they'd witnessed in Philadelphia. This was no longer just a pie-in-the-sky vision from the mouth of a person they'd never met before. It was something they'd now seen with their own eyes!

And it was persuasive. One by one, the partners grew committed to adopting the Practice Growth Model and the attendant approach Alex had laid out at the summit. (As Joe reported all this in private conversation with Alex, he learned that the partners' conversion would likely proceed according to a bell curve first described by Everett Rogers in

1962.[1] They'd had perhaps 15 percent of the partners firmly on their side following the summit and would likely have 75 to 80 percent in the fold within the next few months. All but a few laggards would fall into line within a year.)

When Charles rotated off the executive committee in January, the partners decided Matthew was the logical replacement, given the level of knowledge he'd developed during his visit to Philadelphia. The new executive committee put in long hours, ratifying Joe's choices for segment leaders and finalizing the compensation plan linking pay to performance.

The biggest fly in the ointment lay in the audit department. Then, in early January, Crandall & Potter was the beneficiary of an enormous and completely unexpected boon. A shift in strategy at Pricewaterhouse-Coopers left a young audit dynamo, Philip Van Landingham, on the lookout for new possibilities. A partner in Alex's firm mentioned it at lunch one day, adding a hearty endorsement ("I've known this guy since college. What I'd give if we had a place for him!"). Alex excused himself and phoned Joe immediately with the news. Joe then got in touch with Philip right away to feel him out about his level of interest in a position with a Minneapolis firm.

Joe knew, from Alex, that the Weinstein & Federman partner had been telling Philip for years, "The water's terrific over here in a midsize firm." This worked greatly in Joe's favor, as he was able to sketch out the situation at C&P in a way that was appealing to Philip. Joe was honest about Charles's tepid response to the firm's new direction, but emphasized the fact that his technical prowess would be a strong asset in an audit department newly reorganized under Philip.

Philip took a few days to think it over, but he knew instinctively that he craved this kind of challenge. He was excited by the prospect of being in on the ground floor of a firm's transition to the Practice Growth Model. He was also ready for the atmosphere of a midsize firm. Joe met Philip at

---

[1] *Diffusion of Innovations*, 5th Edition, by E.M. Rogers (2003). New York: The Free Press, a Division of Simon & Schuster Adult Publishing Group.

the airport the night before his planned visit to Crandall & Potter, then took him to dinner to map out the approach Philip would take with Charles. The two decided that Philip would need to "sell" the senior audit partner on the idea that, together, they could take the audit department to previously unimagined heights.

The plan worked to perfection. Joe had prepared Charles as well, emphasizing the fact that the goal was to strengthen the audit department by increasing its resources, particularly in light of new opportunities arising from Sarbanes-Oxley. This was a masterly stroke on Joe's part, playing as it did to Charles's enormous pride in his department. Near the end of the conversation, Charles allowed that he'd much rather do technical work anyway, so the idea of having another partner to do the "selling," as he put it, was "not entirely unwelcome."

Thus, when Joe introduced the two men on the day of Philip's visit, it was with a sense of optimism rather than dread.

Philip turned out to be every bit as effective in handling Charles as Joe might have hoped. When Charles ran into Joe a few days later in the lunchroom, he told Joe wonderingly, "You know, Philip may be the first partner—I mean potential partner—who's ever really understood me." Joe swallowed the huge smile that threatened to break out across his face.

Philip's visit to the Minneapolis firm was an unqualified success. He made an excellent impression on all the partners, even Frank, and a consensus was reached very quickly to offer him the position of audit segment leader. Philip accepted the offer, and both sides were bright with anticipation.

So, though Charles was no more interested in the Practice Growth Model than he'd ever been, at least he was no longer actively hostile. He did drop into Joe's office, after a firm-wide e-mail message had spread the glad tidings that Philip would be joining Crandall & Potter, to point out that of course this would change nothing in the way he, Charles, did his job.

"I regard all this as a tempest in a teapot," he said airily. "But until it blows over, I'm willing to do my part." Joe realized that Charles's idea of "doing his part" consisted of not making waves. He was more than content with that.

Even before Philip had officially settled into his new job, he began lobbying Joe to raid his former firm to snatch away a terrific young business developer named Michael Cunningham. Joe pulled the executive committee members into the discussion, and before long Michael was also on a plane to Minneapolis. In a long dinner meeting, Philip and Michael described for Joe, Kevin, Eric, and Matthew an approach they'd developed and refined during their time together at PwC. The response was enthusiastic, and when Michael met with the C&P partners the following day, the executive committee had thrown its full weight behind Michael's candidacy.

He began his new duties a month later, and the contrast with Ty was so pronounced it was almost painful. Michael clearly understood from day one that he had two jobs—to sell externally *and* internally. He also realized that the second job was the more difficult of the two. But, working with the partners, he began to gain their trust as he helped them develop and close business opportunities. His straightforward, professional approach yielded results almost immediately.

The hardest nuts for Michael to crack were Charles and Frank. The milk of Charles's human kindness rained down exclusively on his new audit partner, and he had little use for Michael. Frank went out of his way to nitpick every suggestion Michael made, but, unlike the situation with Ty, he found few who shared his dire views. In time, even Frank's opposition began to wane.

Some Success, Then a Huge Blunder

Michael immediately assumed responsibility for pipeline activity, asking Joe to chair the meetings, but showing him how to do so in such a way that meetings never wandered off course or bogged down. Partners came prepared and gradually grew into the spirit of things. There were no repeats of the pageantry involving Durwood and his Starbucks "notepaper."

Tiff was tasked with driving pipeline metrics and began to show signs of growth. Her first telephone visit with Katherine had left her quaking in her designer boots, but Katherine's encouraging style made it hard for Tiff to stay intimidated for long. "The partners are your clients, Tiffany," she'd explained patiently. "Do you understand that?"

"Not really," Tiff had admitted.

Katherine took the time to explain what Joe had only touched on. "There's so much they must tell you for you to do your job effectively. You must draw this information out of them—information that will enable you to *help them develop business.*

"What constitutes success, from this day forward? A marketing award? No, Tiffany, success comes when a partner bursts into your office, fresh off the phone from finding out that Crandall & Potter won that big contract, in part because of the support *you* provided! You have to make these partners need you!"

Tiff started to express more reservations, but Katherine would have none of it. "If you didn't have it in you, Tiffany, Joe and Alex would have sent you on your way long since. They believe you can do this. So do I. It's really up to you, though."

Katherine had said enough. Tiff picked up her ringing phone that afternoon and found her old buddy Ty on the other end of the line. He'd called to commiserate—he was having trouble landing another job on par with the one he'd lost—and he wanted Tiff's sympathy. More than that, he wanted her to join him in criticizing Joe and the C&P partners.

To her surprise, Tiff was offended. She wanted no part in running down this firm. She realized then that she'd made her choice. The die was cast. She was moving forward.

Tiff began working closely with Michael as he sized up—uncannily, it sometimes seemed—the highest-odds opportunities, then helped the partners pursue them. Things seemed to be going well, but then disaster struck. Durwood got a hot lead on a huge insurance prospect, and everyone wanted part of the action. Michael tried to impose reason, pointing out that Crandall & Potter had no experience in insurance work. His calls, though, fell on deaf ears.

Six days after the insurance prospect hit the pipeline, a handsome lead surfaced in construction—a Crandall & Potter specialty—but, strangely, no one seemed very interested in working on that one. It didn't help that it was Joshua's lead, since Joshua was, though a very able accountant, very quiet, the least dynamic member of the firm. Durwood had the greatest experience in construction, but he was busy helping write the insurance proposal, and Joshua couldn't engage his interest.

Still, this was a field in which C&P had real, demonstrated strength! It made no sense to pursue the insurance lead to the exclusion of this one! So Michael begged for help with the construction opportunity, but with so many caught up in the potential insurance work, no one had a moment to spare for anything else. In the end, Joshua's only help came from Michael. The two men worked long hours and brought Tiff in as well. ("Poor Tiff," Michael told Joshua. "She's pulled two ways and doesn't get to choose sides like you partners did.")

As the three were lingering one night over an empty pizza box, putting the finishing touches on the proposal, Joshua turned to Michael and Tiff, a curious expression on his face. "You both know how much I appreciate your help on this, right?" Seeing two nods, he went on. "Well, I feel like I have to say something. Even though we've knocked ourselves out on this opportunity, I just don't have the best feeling about how it's going to turn out.

"We've been really under the gun on this thing, basically ever since we learned about it. I just question whether, with the time constraints we've had, we've been able to uncover the hidden agendas of the decision makers on this one . . . plus the politics that always play a part. You know what I mean, Michael. You've been preaching it since you got here."

"You must have been listening, even if other people weren't." The business developer softened his words with a smile. "I do know what you mean, Joshua, and I can't say I disagree with you. There are always key needs—personal and professional—that play a deciding role in these things. We didn't have time to ferret them out; you're right about that. I wish we had. We gave it our best shot, though, with the resources we had, and if we lose it, it isn't your loss, or mine. It's the firm's, in the deepest sense of the word." He drew a deep breath, shrugged, and the conversation moved on.

The exchange seemed to draw a line under the closeness these three had developed while working on the opportunity. They may not have felt particularly pleased with or proud of what they'd been able to cobble together, but they were proud of the work they'd done together in difficult circumstances. They all believed it would stand them in good stead in the future.

The day came, though, when a pall fell over the firm. The insurance business was to be awarded on a Wednesday afternoon, and many of the partners had already gathered in the lunchroom, planning a small celebration of their expected triumph. Joe appeared in the door, hands in his pockets, a hard-to-read expression on his face.

The suspense didn't last long. "Well, people, bad news," he said brutally. "You lost the insurance proposal." Only Michael noticed his use of the word "you" instead of "we."

"No way!" Ben sang out. "We had that one in the bag! We worked our behinds off on that one! How could we lose it?"

"It went to Cornell & Framingham," Joe said. "Guess what? They specialize in insurance. Been doing it for fifty years."

He turned on his heel to depart, wanting to get out of the room before something intemperate slipped out of his mouth. He'd seen the circus atmosphere building around the insurance proposal, and Michael had talked with him about the cold shoulder he and Joshua had gotten on the construction work. Joe knew he'd have to tackle all this, but he wanted to do it in the proper setting.

But as he started through the door, he nearly bumped into Joshua, who was entering the room with an absent look on his face. "Hey, watch out," Joe said. "You look like you could walk into a wall without noticing."

"Sorry," Joshua said, the look on his face spelling misery. "I just got some very disappointing news. The construction work went to another firm."

Joe could feel the steam rising in his head. "Why?" he asked shortly.

The younger partner moved his shoulders in frustration. "From what they told me, they thought the proposal didn't uncover all their needs, didn't display a proper understanding of their business. So what could they expect from us on the work itself?"

"That's it!" Joe snapped, spinning on his heel to face the group of partners. "We'll meet tomorrow morning at nine to discuss this calamity. Everyone who can be there, great. Everyone who can't, we'll fill you in later." He strode from the room abruptly, leaving a group of glum and grumpy CPAs in his wake.

At nine o'clock the following morning, eighteen of the partners were present, either in person or by phone, along with Tiff, Michael, and Jackie. "I think we all know the situation by now," Joe began crisply. "We had two big opportunities in hand. One was in insurance, which we know next to nothing about. The other was in construction, a field where we're acknowledged leaders and where we have a focus on building the niche. For some reason, the insurance opportunity was the sexier of the two, and three-quarters of the partners fell in love with it. Joshua, Michael, and Tiff labored alone on the construction opportunity.

"Well, you all know what happened. We lost the insurance work because we didn't know the field. We lost the construction opportunity because we didn't have the time to really understand the hidden buyer motivation and politics—and, really, how could we, with only one partner and a piece of a business developer and marketer available to work on it?"

Joe rapped hard on the table with his knuckles. "Take my word for it, ladies and gentlemen, this will not happen again at Crandall & Potter— not on my watch. From now on, we're going to be true to our pipeline priorities, and we're going to provide organization and structure to support our revenue segmentation work.

"For pipeline priorities, that means focusing on the opportunities that offer the best chance for a return. For revenue segments, it means focusing on the segments that we've determined have the highest overall priority in this firm. So, from here on out, our decisions will *never again be made willy nilly*—on the pipeline *or* segment side. We'll develop the opportunities we've selected and focus on the segments we've targeted.

"For a little more detail on all this," Joe concluded, "I've asked Michael, first, to address the issue of pipeline priorities."

"My part is pretty simple," Michael said. He went on to explain that, henceforth, all potential opportunities would be evaluated through the pipeline process before *any* work began to try to win the opportunity. Once he'd outlined that, he concluded, "On the segment side, which probably needs more fleshing out, Joe asked the executive committee members to fill you in."

Old Dogs, New Tricks

Eric nodded to Michael and turned to the group. "I'll start. Joe asked Kevin, Matthew, and me to explain this because it's something we saw in action during our visit to Philadelphia. It's a terrific approach to managing leads, and all of us were impressed with it." He glanced at his two fellow executive members, who were nodding agreement.

"The genius of revenue segmentation is that it, well, 'slices and dices' a firm's revenue streams and puts them all on a simple spreadsheet. I made up a dummy as an example, and I'm going to pass it around now."

Revenue Segmentation

Industries ➡	Industry	Industry	Industry	General	Total	% of Total
Service Lines	Banking	Hospitality	Construct			
Assurance	$360	$1,250	$460	$120	$2,190	37%
General Practice	$120	$230	$560	$240	$1,150	20%
Tax	$650	$470	$380	$240	$1,740	30%
Lit Support	$180	$310	$170	$140	$800	14%
Totals	$1,310	$2,260	$1,570	$740	$5,880	100%
% of Total	22%	38%	27%	13%	100%	

When everyone had a copy, Eric went on. "As you can see, the service lines of the firm are listed down the left side of the grid, and the industries are listed across the top. So we can see at a glance, for instance, that this firm has $360,000 worth of business in assurance work in the banking industry. Everybody with me so far?" Heads bobbed up and down, and he continued.

"We can also see, by looking at the figures to the right and along the bottom, exactly how each segment stacks up in this firm—again, by industry and by service line. So this firm's biggest industry is hospitality, at thirty-eight percent, and their largest segment is assurance, at thirty-seven. Finally, this gives us a snapshot overview of the interrelationships between the firm's revenue sources. Their single biggest revenue segment by far is assurance work in hospitality, with a million and a quarter in revenue. This is one segment that you can safely believe this mythical firm—if it existed—would never neglect." He smiled.

"Now," Eric went on, "we add a little more information." He picked up another stack of spreadsheets and passed them around.

Revenue Segmentation

Industries ➡	Industry	Industry	Industry	General	Total	% of Total	Ptr
Service Lines	Banking	Hospitality	Construct				Leader
Assurance	$360	$1,250	$460	$120	$2,190	37%	John
General Practice	$120	$230	$560	$240	$1,150	20%	Patrick
Tax	$650	$470	$380	$240	$1,740	30%	Sue
Lit Support	$180	$310	$170	$140	$800	14%	Mark
Totals	$1,310	$2,260	$1,570	$740	$5,880	100%	
% of Total	22%	38%	27%	13%	100%		
Partner Leader	Carol	Sam	Jack	Paul			

"This is the same spreadsheet, but now we've added the partner in the firm who's the leader in each segment. So, in the firm's biggest segment, Sam is in charge of hospitality, and John heads up assurance work. Still with me?" More nods.

"Great. Kevin will take over here."

Kevin cleared his throat. "Now that you understand how the information is tracked, I'll tell you what they do with it—not at this fictional firm, but at Alex's. First, they use it as a decision-making tool. Which market segments should they pursue? Which service lines merit efforts in innovation and efficiency? They have an ironclad policy there—one we could have used just now—that they actively pursue leads only in fields where they have a segment leader and a stated commitment. So our ill-fated foray into insurance opportunities wouldn't, *couldn't*, have happened there—unless there were other, very good reasons."

He paused for a look at Joe. "Couldn't have happened *here*, had we had this system in place." Joe nodded, in both agreement and appreciation.

"Second," Kevin went on, "they use this spreadsheet as a communications tool. It not only encourages partners to talk to each other, it makes it instantly obvious who needs to be consulted on any new opportunity. So nothing falls through the cracks anymore.

"Segment leaders hold meetings that are basically strategy sessions, where they study the issues and impediments to growth in their segments at any particular time. The advantages to this are obvious, as different segments face different challenges. Also, the partners don't work at cross purposes, they work together. To see how it works exactly, if we look to the example of our mythical firm, we see that Mark and Carol might get together to develop a strategy for increasing the firm's litigation work in the banking industry. Right?" He looked up, to more nods.

"Fine. Now, there are eleven steps that have been mapped out for building a segment in a service line or niche. We'll get to those details later on, but I want to give you a sense right now of how it works. At the beginning, of course, the work is very basic; the first step is to analyze the revenue stream in the service line or industry niche. Then you execute a research call program, which results in mapping out your strategy for growth, looking at things like market conditions, issues and solutions, channels of distribution, competition, and so forth. There are guidelines for how to do this as well, and we'll make sure all our segment leaders are trained in this, of course. Most of us CPAs have never been exposed to product management, and apparently this is stuff we're going to need to learn.

"The point is that it can get pretty interesting," Kevin concluded, enthusiasm in his voice, "and while we were in Philly, we saw a doozy. Matthew is going to tell you about it."

Matthew smiled and leaned forward. "We got to sit in on a meeting of the assurance service line and construction industry niche. They were cooking up a new offering, one that falls under the ninth stage of segment building—developing innovative offerings—in the model Kevin just told you about.

"The assurance people in Alex's firm had wanted to increase the firm's presence in fraud work, and they knew fraud is a huge problem in the construction industry. So they decided to stop chasing small fraud jobs here and there and team up with the construction partners to go after the huge market they knew existed there.

"One of the Weinstein partners knew a guy whose construction company had just been victimized by fraud, to the tune of over half a million dollars." Matthew paused briefly as a few whistles rent the air. "Right. So Susan, Alex's assurance leader, and Jack, the construction guy, got together and formulated their approach, down to the last detail. Then they got in touch with the guy who'd lost the half mil. What they asked him was simple: Could they apply their model to what had happened at his company, to see if their approach would have detected and thus prevented the fraud?

"Although the construction owner wasn't a client of Alex's firm, he knew of them through his friend, and he figured, Why not? So he said yes. And guess what? Alex's people determined that they *would* have found the fraud, and they were able to demonstrate exactly *how*. At the meeting we sat in on, they were refining the presentation of their findings to this owner and putting together a proposal to protect him from future fraud.

"It was fascinating, I'll tell you that," Matthew concluded. "There was such an intense sense of excitement! We even got into the spirit, although it wasn't our firm. There's something really exhilarating about working with like-minded, really bright people toward a common goal. I think," Matthew added slowly, "if I may offer my own personal observation, that that's what tried to happen here with that insurance bid we just lost. Some of us got so excited about moving into a new field—after all, all we'd heard about lately was growth, growth, and more growth—that we forgot that it has to be *targeted* growth, and none of it can be random."

"You left out the best part," Kevin prompted.

"Oh, right." Matthew laughed. "I talked with Jack yesterday morning. He called to tell me the construction owner was bowled over by their presentation, and he's signed on as a new client. Not only that, he's given Weinstein permission to use his case in their presentations to future prospects. That's what this approach can do for a firm."

"I'm interested, as usual, in the nitty gritty," said Smith. "How are these segment meetings set up? Who comes to them?"

Eric responded. "Generally speaking, segment meetings are scheduled regularly, and usually take place once a month. At first, as Kevin said, the tasks are simple: Quantify the segment and pin down the details, set a revenue goal, decide whether or not there are others in your firm you want to involve, then launch a research call program as a foundation for developing the segment.

"You use all that information to determine your strategy. After that, it's a matter of implementation—first, implementing what you've put in place, and then later updating the segment to keep it fresh and account for new wrinkles in the field. This might consist of refining what you've got, but sometimes you'll be developing entirely new offerings, as Jack and Susan did with fraud."

"And who's involved?" Smith asked again.

"Oh, yes," Eric said. "Generally, it's the segment leaders and maybe their seconds in command. Plus the business developer and marketing director."

"A lot seems to revolve around the segment leaders," Smith observed. "We've been hearing about segment leaders for months now, it seems. When are we going to actually get some?"

Joe rose from his seat, smiling. "I think that's where I come in," he said. "I'd been planning to call a partners' meeting next week to talk about segment leaders, but I think doing it now makes more sense.

"There are two related elements," he said, ticking them off on his fingers. "One is increased responsibility, and the other is increased compensation. Kevin, Eric, and Matthew have worked slavishly to adapt the compensation plan Alex's firm uses for our purposes, and they completed that task a few days ago." Joe went on to explain that they had then worked with him to put the final touches on the list of proposed segment leaders.

"I'm going to ask many of you to rise to the occasion," he said. "For those of you who are already de facto leaders of your segments, this is your chance to become acknowledged leader, and to reap the rewards of that leadership.

"But no one wants to force you to take on this responsibility," he emphasized. "Becoming a segment leader at Crandall & Potter is a sign of distinction, an opportunity to contribute to something great that's going on at the firm. But if you've been the leader in your segment thus far and you don't want this added responsibility, we'll find another partner to take it on. You can be an individual contributor and be paid accordingly. Still, those who step up and help lead the firm will be rewarded.

"Jackie's in the process of putting the new compensation plan on paper, and we'll get together again in a few days to go over it in detail. But for now, those of you who've been leaders in your segments should start thinking it over. We'll be talking with you individually over the next week to ten days. Be ready."

Joe, Kevin, Eric, and Matthew were pleased with the reception they received when they started making these calls. Most potential segment leaders felt honored, and only a few expressed any real reservation. When the process was complete, several segment leaders were in place, representing the areas the firm considered its highest priorities. The new compensation program began to be phased in as well, tying part of segment leaders' incentive compensation to growth within their segments.

"It Works! It Really Works!"

Joe appointed Eric to head up the industry niche portion of the Practice Growth Model and put Kevin in charge of service line management. He encouraged them both to share what they'd learned in Philadelphia, and touched base with them frequently to check in on their progress.

What amazed both Eric and Kevin was how much the Practice Growth Model changed the way they went about their own jobs—and even their perceptions of the jobs themselves. Eric reported that, using the Model, he was now able to plan more strategically, to develop and enhance new offerings in health care.

Moreover, Eric's past success in generating significant growth in his own niche served as a powerful in-house example of the effectiveness of the Practice Growth Model. "Everything I've been doing all along is part of the Model," he kept saying, seemingly amazed by his own prescience. "I just didn't know it had a name!" There wasn't a soul at Crandall & Potter who was unaware of Eric's previous accomplishments, and this success story provided both motivation and reinforcement.

The effect of the Model on Kevin's tax work was even more pronounced. All his past efforts in tax, his service line, had taken place in stage four of the rainmaking process, service delivery. Now he had a blueprint for using all four steps of the rainmaking process, and he threw himself into the effort with a vengeance. He met with the segment leaders of the newly identified industry niches and brainstormed with them to figure out how to apply the firm's tax expertise in their industry. Thus, Kevin began establishing a network of interrelationships that would serve as the template for the other service lines.

The effect on the firm as a whole was electric, as one person after another bought in to the new system, swayed by Joe's burgeoning knowledge and leadership, Eric's in-house demonstration of the Model's effectiveness, and Kevin's enthusiasm and commitment. Barely six months following the strategic summit, the atmosphere at C&P had already changed to the point where the naysayers were beginning to feel out of place, rather than the go-getters. "We're getting there," Joe liked to say whenever given half a chance. "We're making progress. We're on our way."

At a partners' meeting a few weeks later, Joe, Kevin, and Matthew burst through the door almost ten minutes late, huge smiles plastered all over their faces. "You'll never believe it!" Matthew sang out, beaming, slapping the back of a chair. "You'll never believe how beautifully this thing works!"

The three collapsed into chairs, all smiles, as the partners' eyes settled on Joe. "No, I want Kevin and Matthew to tell you about it," he said.

Matthew and Kevin grinned at each other, and Matthew gestured to the more senior partner. "You start."

"Here's what happened," Kevin said, leaning forward on his elbows. "Remember all those warnings from Joe about 'gang warfare'—where partners 'gang up' on first calls to prospects, going in in teams of two or three? According to the Model, this is basically a waste of time, right? But who really knows, because we've never tried it. Then Joe issues his ukase—no more gang warfare, no matter what.

"So Matt and I *have* to try it Joe's way, the Practice Growth Model way. Matt had this lead for a new manufacturing prospect, and he and I cooked up an approach to exploit a tax vulnerability we thought they had. So we decided to do it the Practice Growth Model way, which told us to 'divide and conquer'—you know, split up the key decision makers and see them one on one.

"Well, this is a big company that makes a zillion different electronic components. They've got a couple of subsidiaries, so there's plenty of room for us to spread out. Matt and I made appointments to see two division heads—that is, he saw one guy and I saw the other, in separate meetings—and at the same time Joe set up a time to meet with the CEO. Well, the meetings Matt and I had were okay, we got some good information, and it looks like it's worth pursuing. That's what we decided when we left and touched base.

"But then here comes Joe, and he hit the proverbial jackpot!" Kevin turned to the MP. "You've gotta tell them this part; you earned it."

A broad smile creased Joe's face as he acknowledged the compliment. "It's simple," he said. "The CEO spilled his guts. We started out talking about tax and audit issues, and before you know it, he's telling me about all this other stuff they've been struggling with. They've got estate planning and intergenerational needs—just loads of stuff we never heard about; would never have known to ask about.

"And you can bet it didn't come up in the meetings with the division heads. It wouldn't have come up at all with more people in the room; it was too personal."

Joe turned to Kevin and Matthew for corroboration. "It works, guys!" Matthew said. "If we needed some kind of confirmation that we're on the right track, we got it today in spades. This thing really works!"

Weeks passed, then stretched into months. With Michael spearheading the pipeline process, Joe driving the pipeline reviews, and Eric and Kevin riding herd on segment leaders, inefficiencies in the firm that had previously gone unnoticed began to take on a radioactive pall. It was becoming very clear where the firm's besetting problems lay: The partners were too busy to prospect, so they sat on their hands and waited for new business to come to them. When they had a new lead, they put too much emphasis on the proposal instead of the pursuit. The difference was that, in the past, such behavior was the norm. Now it drew attention immediately, and Michael, Kevin, Eric, Tiff, and Joe joined forces to nudge—or, sometimes, push—partners in the right direction.

Little by little, the results began to pile up. And every so often, there was a huge "aha!" moment, like the time Joe, Kevin, and Matthew came storming back, triumphant, from the firm's first "divide and conquer" mission. There were signs that the Model was working. The firm's win rate on new opportunities began to edge upward.

Moving Up, Moving Down

One Tuesday afternoon in September, Joe looked up as Tiff strode into his office. He smiled at her, marveling again at the rapid transformation she'd undergone. How had Katherine managed to teach Tiff so much in such a short time? How had Tiff managed to assimilate it all? If Joe hadn't known better, he'd have sworn this was a new person, this Tiff Hollister who stood before him now. Could he even remember the last time she'd gotten sidetracked on some irrelevant project?

These days, her work was sharply focused. She undertook nothing that wasn't directly related to achieving the firm's revenue objectives, and she invariably considered the revenue effect before proposing anything new. The partners were beginning to trust her, and even the older, more staid ones were starting to include her in their planning sessions without being told.

"I'm proud of you, Tiff," Joe said abruptly, then stopped, embarrassed.

"Thanks, Joe," Tiff replied, sinking down into a chair. "I think I know what you mean. We've come a long way, haven't we?"

"We have," Joe allowed. "You know, the thought that crossed my mind when you came in the door was, How did you do it so fast? Change, that is."

Tiff thought for a moment. "I think it was really just a paradigm shift," she said. "Katherine made it clear, very clear, *overwhelmingly* clear, that the things I'd been taught to hold dear—branding, marketing/communications, and all that other tactical stuff—were just the means to an end, not the end itself. The end—the aim—is growth. She also taught me how to think strategically. I'm still learning, of course, but if I run across something I don't understand, or that feels unfamiliar, I know who to pick up the phone and call. Katherine's been incredibly generous with her time, not to mention her expertise."

"Alex tells me Katherine says you're one of the quickest studies she's ever seen."

"She's a good teacher," Tiff replied modestly. "We've all come a long way, haven't we, Joe? A year ago, the partners didn't want me cluttering up their annual meeting. I think they'd feel differently today."

"I know they would," Joe said warmly. "You've put an enormous amount of time and energy into learning the Model. Even the best teacher is sunk if the pupil isn't up to the challenge. So don't try to downplay the effort you put in."

"All right. I agree that it's been hard work, but more than that, in some ways it was really scary, wasn't it—for all of us?"

Joe nodded. "Change is always hard. Major change, like this, can be terrifying." He smiled. "Don't think you were the only one who felt it. But I meant it earlier when I said I'm proud of you."

He shifted in his chair. "Still, something tells me you didn't come here to collect kudos. What's up?"

Tiff described the situation bluntly. "It's Frank," she said. "He's become a real problem, and I think it's going to require your involvement."

"Tell me about it," Joe said, then sat back to listen to a précis of the problem at hand, most of which he already knew. Frank had been named segment leader for real estate, a niche he'd led in a de facto way for years. He'd talked a good game at the beginning, but it had become gnawingly clear over the past few months that he had no intention of ever doing things the Practice Growth Model way.

"He knows the drill, and he couldn't care less," Tiff said. At segment leader meetings, where each segment leader was supposed to bring one or, at most, two trusted assistants, Frank would show up with eight or nine people, including junior-level staff who were completely extraneous at such a meeting. "And they all sit around the table taking up space," Tiff explained, "and they have no earthly idea what they're there for.

"I've talked with Frank," she went on. "Eric's talked with him. I personally have had probably five or six conversations about the problem, and I know Michael's dealt with Frank privately as well. He knows what the expectations are, but he just doesn't get it—or doesn't want to get it; I don't know. But I do know he's dragging the segment down, and to a certain extent dragging down other segments that have to work with him on cross-segment projects."

"Is that it?" Joe asked.

"Well, no," Tiff admitted. "I guess my frustration is showing, and I apologize for that. But I just came out of a meeting with him, and it makes me want to chew glass. I was sitting there at the table with him and nine—*nine!*—of his minions, and I was trying to work with him to define his segment, so we can get moving on the right strategy.

"Well, I'm trying to pin him down. 'What kinds of entities are we targeting?' I ask. And he sidesteps the question, and I try again. So we keep dancing around like this for maybe twenty minutes, and finally he draws himself up, and he looks down his nose at me, and he says, 'Where's that brochure you promised me six weeks ago?'

"Joe, even if we were still doing brochures right and left, how could we possibly develop one for a segment that has no definition? So I was irked. But I remembered what Katherine told me—never throw up your hands and walk out. Instead, I said, very calmly, 'Frank, there's no question of a brochure until the segment is fleshed out.'

"Well, at that point, Josie spoke up"— Josie Fitzmorris was a manager who was probably six months away from making partner, an up-and-coming talent with enormous potential—"and she said several of the staff had come up with some ideas, and maybe we could kick them around for a while and see if there was anything there."

Tiff shook her head at the memory. "And, Joe, you should have seen Frank turn on her! I'd seen him do that kind of thing before—put her down big time when she offered any kind of suggestion—but this time he really lit into her. He'd been pleasant to her earlier in the meeting, but he turned on her in a trice once she spoke up."

Tiff paused thoughtfully. "You know, it's kind of funny. He wants to play king of the hill—that's why he drags all those juniors along with him to meetings—yet he won't listen to a thing they have to say. Their role is to sit there and say nothing, to nod respectfully when he speaks.

Heaven forfend that they should have an idea, much less one that's better than his."

Joe leaned back and surveyed his marketing—soon to be practice growth—director. "Have you ever talked with Josie outside of the meetings?"

"Sure. We ran into each other in the lunchroom last week and got to talking."

"And?"

"Well, she does have ideas, and some of them definitely merit consideration. She's clearly familiar with the strengths the firm has in this segment, and she has some very specific ideas about which things it makes the most sense to go after.

"We talked about the Model some, too, and it's obvious that she understands how it works on a practical basis. We kicked around some ideas about STP and lead generation, and she was tossing out ways to work with Kevin on large opportunity development and management within the niche."

"Sounds to me like *she* should be segment leader," Joe said.

"I'll tell you," Tiff said, "I think she could do it."

And so it came to pass. After two meetings with Frank, it was clear to Joe that Frank didn't have it in him to head up this niche. After five minutes with Josie, it was clear that she did.

The news that Frank had been replaced as segment leader by a freshly minted partner shook Crandall & Potter, and Joe made a point of doing two things. First, he introduced Josie at her first partner's meeting, making it clear that the entire weight of his leadership was firmly behind her. He talked about the new culture of effectiveness now in place at the firm. "Those who contribute to the success of Crandall & Potter will be rewarded," he said simply. "Those who lead their segments *effectively* will be rewarded."

Second, he talked privately with Frank, making it clear that he would gain no advantage by trying to make waves. "Welcome her," Joe said simply. "Act like it was your idea, that you wanted out. You can save face and help the firm at the same time. But the decision is final," he added cautionarily. "If you choose to make waves, it won't be Josie who drowns."

By late fall, revenue segment efforts under the new system were well under way. Gone were the old methods: mailing lists, brochures, ineffective direct-mail letters. In their place was a system that combined researching the ecosystem, developing strategy, and making well-planned and well-executed research and opportunity development calls.

The new approach had been fleshed out in a partners' meeting led by Michael. "Today we're going to explore a highly effective method of developing a referral system called 'researching the ecosystem.' I know you've all heard this phrase more than once, and today you'll learn exactly what it means and how to use the approach effectively," Michael began. He went on to explain how traditional means of seeking referrals—networking through Rotary or Chamber of Commerce meetings, or lunching with bankers and lawyers—typically produced limited results. "It's hard to stand out from the crowd," Michael explained, "when you are, in fact, one of the crowd.

"There's a better way, and it revolves around building and maintaining an ongoing program of *research calls*—meaning face-to-face meetings within specific vertical 'ecosystems.' That means your industry niches," Michael added. This approach, he explained, offered several advantages, which he ticked off on his fingers. It helped CPAs improve their understanding of the nature of the business within a specific target niche. It heightened the firm's visibility among desired prospects. It helped the firm craft an effective strategy to differentiate itself in the marketplace. And it brought the firm's partners face to face with potential buyers.

C&P partners would be targeting four distinct groups, Michael explained:

1. Thought leaders (association heads, editors, writers, speakers, and the like)

2. "Providers" to a target niche (not only traditional attorneys, bankers, insurance brokers, and others who were *firmly* established within a desired niche, but also providers of *any* goods and services to that niche)

3. Likely buyers (including current clients and *perfectly profiled* prospects)

4. Competitors (to help the firm understand how to differentiate as well as to identify where "big fish" dominate and where market holes exist)

"This system has many strengths," Michael went on, "including, first and maybe most important, the fact that it does *not* involve actually asking for business—ever. You're asking for *information*, instead, and that should feel completely natural to you and unintimidating to the person you're talking with.

"Second, these meetings can take place whenever you want, so they're not tied to a calendar, and they don't tie you to a schedule. Just plan two meetings a week, and in a year, you'll have made a hundred research calls!

"Third, as you do this over time, you'll build up a terrific lead base, one you'll be adding to with each new conversation. Don't ever leave a meeting without collecting at least two new names. The last question you ask in every conversation should probably be, 'Which other thought leaders in this niche should I get in touch with?' Even after you've researched your niche completely, you'll continue to inventory contacts within your four categories . . . you remember, thought leaders and so forth.

"And remember, your goal at all times is to learn everything you can about the 'ecosystem'—the niche—you're swimming in. As your knowledge of it fills up with new content and ideas, you may start to think about new offerings or gain insight into reconstituting current ones.

"That's terrific, and it's evidence that the system is working. Because leads are actually a by-product of this process, not the goal. Still, if you're in a market that's potentially fertile, and you give this system a try and keep at it for a period of months, you'll see results. You'll have lots of new leads, and the path to refining current offerings and developing new ones will become clear."

Growing Pains, Then More Growth

As the first anniversary of the adoption of the Model drew near, the changes at Crandall & Potter were almost palpable. Tiff was focused and effective in her work, and the partners increasingly looked to her for vital support in their growth efforts.

It was also abundantly clear that, in hiring Michael Cunningham as business developer, the firm had finally backed a winner. Michael made the partners stick to best practices, and although he was unfailingly polite and professional, he made it clear at all times that he meant business.

He also had a way of bringing ideas home to the CPAs in ways they could grasp immediately. "Executing opportunity development badly is like doing a shabby audit or tax project—you'll get bad results, plain and simple," he said.

Joe's leadership of the firm's pipeline was showing results as well. He employed positive peer pressure to maintain enthusiasm among the partners, taking the time to send personal e-mail messages congratulating each team when it scored a win.

And the wins were coming more often now. When they didn't come, when the firm lost an opportunity, Michael treated it as a learning experience rather than an embarrassment. "Even the best rainmakers can fail sometimes, just as Torii Hunter can fall down chasing a fly ball," Michael said, referencing the man who'd been a perennial All-Star center fielder for the Twins. "Hey, he's still one of the best in the game. The point is that he doesn't hide in the dugout after a failure. He learns from the experience and goes back out there and keeps competing.

"And that's what we'll do."

The firm had achieved greater visibility and was beginning to make inroads in new segments they had targeted, including SAS 70 and manufacturing, where Matthew had assumed the mantle of leadership. There was change in the air in construction, where it was beginning to appear that Joshua would likely be taking over as segment leader, a post currently held by Durwood. Durwood had been a solid, if unexceptional, de facto leader in years past, but he was beginning to agree with his pal Frank that being a segment leader wasn't all it was cracked up to be—so much work, and all of it so new, and hey, why not let a young whipper-snapper like Joshua take the lead and sort out all the newfangled notions?

Joe always smiled when he heard such emotions expressed. Following Frank's deferral to Josie in the real estate segment, Durwood would be the second segment leader to step aside, ceding the post to a younger, hungrier partner. All these changes took place with Joe's full blessing. And he managed to engineer the transitions in such a way that no one lost face openly. Though Joe didn't think much about it at the time, he was growing, too—as a leader.

SAS 70 and manufacturing were beginning to look like winners, and construction would be on a sounder footing soon, but other segments were slower to develop. Segment meetings continued to consume time and energy, as the messy but critical work of hammering out effective strategies and evaluating tactical execution in previously neglected segments continued. The segment leaders were learning important product management concepts. Moreover, after they figured out where they were in the life cycle of their segments, they were able to diagnose what was missing. Then, working with Michael and Tiff, they honed in on specific problems, identifying opportunities, and focusing with deadly accuracy on those problems and opportunities.

Probably the most popular meeting was "Show & Tell," in which segment leaders met for a day to display and share their work. And, *mirabile dictu*, the partners made actual connections to each other's work throughout the day, as one partner would begin, "Kevin and I are working on the issue of . . . " or "Smith and I are collaborating on an opportunity in . . . " And then the partners not only knew where others were focusing, but were free to contribute if they could. And they did.

"So many connections!" Matthew marveled at the end of one such Show & Tell session. "There are so many good things happening around here!"

"Right," Kevin said succinctly. "And we don't waste time anymore sitting around telling each other, 'We should take a look at X'—and then it never goes anywhere. It's a whole new ball game around here; that's the truth."

Still, with all the progress, there were inevitably times when frustrations boiled over. "I feel like we're in the middle of a cyclone!" Joe told Michael one day. "There's so much going on, it feels almost overwhelming sometimes."

"I know," Michael acknowledged in his low-key manner. "But just how long, again, were these segments neglected?"

"I know," Joe said, sighing. "I realize we can't straighten it out overnight, and I know it'll all be worth it in the end. But right now, it feels like utter chaos."

"Ask your wife," Michael said with a smile. "Ask Becky. Ask her what it's like to fix Christmas dinner. I think it's just like this—controlled chaos. But it's worth it in the end. And if you don't go through it, you won't have the delicious meal to enjoy. After all," he added with a smile, "you can't go out to a restaurant and order up a new segment group. You've gotta cook it at home, mess and all."

One sunny April afternoon in year two of the new regime, Eric walked into Joe's office and found himself in the midst of a party—well, call it a celebration. Matthew, Tiff, Michael, and Joe were standing around toasting each other with soft drink cans, and the room was awash with smiles.

"I miss something?" Eric asked. "Somebody died and left Mayo Clinic to us?"

"Ha!" Matthew said. "You jest. But it's just about that good." Eric could hardly believe his eyes. Here was Matthew—staid, earnest, buttoned-down Matthew—looking positively ebullient. "You know we've been chasing Martin-David Industries," Matthew said, naming one of the premier manufacturing firms in the Twin City area.

"How could I not?" Eric asked. "I've been hearing about it at every pipeline review for the past four months. Don't tell me," he said. "Let me guess. We won?"

"We won!" Matthew said. "Against two other big firms, including Diggs & Carey."

"Wow," Eric breathed. He vividly recalled, as did every partner at Crandall & Potter, how they'd lost out to Diggs & Carey on the Swanson Products opportunity—the big tuna Charles let get away in the early days. "Isn't this, like, $300,000?"

"Yes!" Matthew said proudly. He reached over and grabbed another soda can and handed it to Eric. "So join us in a toast to the best darn large opportunity team in Minneapolis." Everybody smiled, and five Coke and Diet Coke cans clinked in celebration.

By the next pipeline review two days later, Matthew had a partner in celebration. Josie had spearheaded a proposal that pulled out all the stops, including a successful divide-and-conquer foray where Joe again played a pivotal role, to land a major engagement with the second largest real estate broker in the Twin City area. The partners broke into a spontaneous round of applause for Matthew and Josie when the announcement of the two wins was made. Joe made sure Tiff and Michael received their share of the commendation too.

At the end of the meeting, as usual, Michael totted up the current numbers and updated the pipeline status. "Well, ladies and gentlemen, we now stand at one-hundred-fifty leads in our pipeline, and on more than half of them, I'm working closely with the partners. That is significant, folks," he said, looking up. "Joe, how many leads did you have a year and a half ago, at your first pipeline review?"

"Can I claim a faulty memory?" Joe joked, then added, "Just over fifty, I believe."

"We're ahead of schedule on revenue in the pipeline, too," Michael added. "Who can tell me what our goal is for pipeline dollars, in terms of percentage of annual revenue?"

About eight partners spoke at once. "Twenty!" they called out, as the others nodded.

"You're good," Michael smiled. "We expected to hit twenty percent at the two-year point, but we're almost there already, with 18 percent, after only a year and a half. Folks, that's terrific news. You all are doing it, you are launching this firm into the big leagues!"

Twelve weeks later, at the quarterly account review meeting, Joe noticed another major change. Segment leaders were starting to behave as their titles implied; they were actually beginning to *lead*. When a new opportunity came in, the partner who headed it up knew exactly which segment leader to turn to for support—and the support was starting to be there, reliably and effectively.

Then, barely one month later, there was another coup. On Alex's advice, Joe had instituted a firm-wide monthly teleconference meeting that, rather than crushing partners and staff beneath a load of statistics, turned on recognizing achievements and celebrating wins. In addition to the camaraderie and mutual support these meetings engendered, the meetings underscored a new system of rewarding outstanding work. Most of the rewards were relatively modest—a night on the town, or tickets to a sporting or cultural event—but there were cash bonuses as well for truly outstanding achievements.

One C&P manager cashed in big at the August meeting. One of the Big Four accounting firms had been forced by a conflict of interest to bow out of a major project for a large public company. The Crandall & Potter team, led by Philip, in close collaboration with Michael and Tiff, won the $500,000 opportunity, setting off the biggest celebration yet.

"It feels like old times," Michael told Philip.

"No, it's better," Philip said. "Everything my pal told me about working in a medium-size firm is true. There's more flexibility, more room for personal growth, and there's every bit as much action."

"You know, you're right," Michael reflected. "I'm glad you brought me here."

Happy as Philip, Michael, and Tiff were, the manager who'd heard about the opportunity and tipped Philip off was probably the happiest. Her pay envelope carried the weight of a $10,000 bonus that month. She wasn't the only one who was enthused, though. With the chance to pull down that kind of bonus, what right-minded person wouldn't want to work at Crandall & Potter?

Full Circle

Joe stood alone in his study at home, adjusting the cummerbund of his tuxedo. Tonight was a huge night in the history of Crandall & Potter. The firm was hosting a black-tie dinner for everyone, from the managing partner down to the last mailroom clerk, along with their companions. Alex and Katherine had been invited as well, but Alex said this night belonged to Crandall & Potter.

Three years had passed since that fateful evening when Eric, Kevin, and, through his lack of resistance if nothing more, Charles, had made a decision to change the way C&P did business. Three years later, the firm was scarcely recognizable. Certainly there was almost no remaining resemblance to the group of talented but undisciplined CPAs of three years ago.

Today, Crandall & Potter was well known and acknowledged, not only in Minneapolis but throughout the Midwest, as one of the fastest-growing and most innovative CPA firms in existence. Inwardly, the signs were all positive as well. Growth and net income per partner had grown even faster than they'd hoped in their wildest dreams. Crandall & Potter had become a shining example of the power of the Practice Growth Model. Not a week went by that Joe didn't receive a phone call from the managing partner of some other foundering firm, asking just how, exactly, they did it.

They kept on doing it. The firm's research call program was bringing in new business all the time. And these days, of course, the new business was in segments where Crandall & Potter had a strong focus.

Which is not to say the firm was not branching out into new segments; nothing could be further from the case. Joe and Michael made it a point to work closely with any partner who believed it made sense to break into a new segment. Indeed, there were six more active segments now than there were just 12 months ago. The firm was growing, changing, flourishing.

To keep up with the human resource needs of the ongoing expansion, the firm had hired its first recruiting director, Lisa Olson, ten months ago. These days, Crandall & Potter was always on the lookout for young CPAs or partners in established firms who craved a new challenge. For those who were hard workers and could fit into the Practice Growth Model way of business, there was always a place at Crandall & Potter.

Joe recalled a 20-minute walk he'd taken down the halls earlier in the day. He'd done it just to soak in the atmosphere, to bask in conversations that hummed with intensity and promise. It was hard to go 10 minutes without overhearing at least one reference to the "big fish." Joe chuckled to himself. "Landing the Big Fish" was one of the first workshops Crandall & Potter had held during the transition. The C&P partners had picked up the concept quickly.

Today's walk had brought him into the realm of the manufacturing segment, where Matthew was talking with a newly hired young CPA, hammering home the difference between "significant" opportunities and others. New accountants at C&P were expected to learn the "PGM way" quickly, and almost invariably, they did. Crandall & Potter was a popular target for young CPAs these days, and Lisa had little trouble filling positions at any level.

Later during the walk, Joe had stopped in briefly on a meeting in the audit segment. Charles—*Charles!*—was showing the newest partner how to determine which of a number of competitive strategies was best for a particular prospect. "It won't be the same every time, Rachel," he was explaining patiently. "We have a number of strategies to choose from, and the key is to figure out which one will work *here*. Of course, the only way we learn that is through research—which means, in most cases, meeting with and talking to people. We call it researching the ecosystem."

Joe marveled often these days at the change in Charles. It hadn't happened right away; Charles had given Michael the cold shoulder for many months and found little to work on with Philip. Eventually, though, he'd started coming around, reassured by the unfailing respect he received from Philip and Michael, and piqued by their results. Charles and Philip worked together smoothly now, Joe knew, with Michael remaining in the background at times. Charles was in fact Philip's most vocal admirer.

Joe had asked Charles about it once, prodding just enough to get a sense of where all the equanimity came from. "Oh, it's very simple," Charles had explained. "It's all a matter of finding your place in the world. My place was never being a rah-rah fellow. I lead by example. And Philip has *his* place. He leads by exhortation." Charles then paused to grin wickedly. "And never the twain shall meet."

Joe continued his stroll, catching snippets of conversations here and there, about triangulation and elongation, what the last round of ecosystem research had turned up that they could never have anticipated, and, here, there, and everywhere, talk of opportunities and more opportunities.

Near the end of his walk, Joe had stood quietly, looking on as Tiff, Michael, and Smith patiently tutored a young CPA, taking a draft presentation he'd prepared and showing the younger man what it *didn't* contain that it should have. "First you ask yourself this," Michael said. " 'What are the prospect's needs?' You have to know enough about the prospect that you can put yourself in his shoes and answer that. If you can't, you're not ready to write the proposal. Because the proposal is a history book, Bruce, not a sales tool. It's an historical record of what you learned in your discussions with the prospect. If you didn't find out enough, then you won't win. It's as simple as that."

Smith picked up the thought. "When you've got all that figured out, you go ahead and prepare the proposal. Then the last step, when you're finished, is to send a draft of the proposal to the prospect and ask him to enhance it. That way, the prospect is in a sense writing the proposal along with you, and he has an emotional investment in its success too."

The young man asked a follow-up question, but Joe drifted off, trolling casually for still more evidence of Crandall & Potter's successful implementation of the enormously effective Practice Growth Model.

Joe had also had a talk with Eric a couple of days ago. The two men had had lunch to celebrate Eric's thirteenth anniversary with the firm, and somehow the conversation meandered onto Old Man Potter. "He left this firm to me," Joe said, "and you know, Eric, that someday I'll leave it to you."

Eric's frank smile showed both appreciation and restraint. "Joe, I'll always be grateful for the confidence you've shown in me. But I hope I won't step into your shoes for a good many years. I don't expect to."

"Don't worry; you won't," Joe said with a laugh. "Seriously, have you ever taken time out to think about your role in all this? You got it all started, you know. You came and told me the partners were about to mutiny."

"You listened," Eric insisted. "You didn't try to stick your head in the sand."

"It's been a lot of hard work," Joe said, "but we did it. We all did. You know, our win rate now is nearly seventy percent. Seventy! If Alex had told us that at the executive committee meeting three years ago, I wouldn't have believed him. Seventy percent!" Joe stopped, and his face took on an air of sober reflection. "It's been one heck of a ride, Eric and, you know, it's not even over yet. In fact, in some ways I feel like we're just getting started."

Joe stepped into the hotel ballroom that Friday evening and glanced about the room at his Crandall & Potter colleagues. Pride rose strongly within his bosom, and for a moment he felt almost overcome with emotion. At his side, Becky felt his response and gave his hand a gentle squeeze. These men and women were resplendent in their finery, completely given over to the joy of celebrating their shared accomplishment.

Joe did not know that his phone would ring tomorrow morning at home, and that he'd find Alex on the other end of the line. He didn't know that Alex would be calling, for the first time ever, really, not to extend a helping hand but to request one. He didn't know that Alex was even now on the phone with his first college roommate, a man he'd been close to for 35 years. His friend was also a CPA and headed a midsize firm in San Francisco. The friend's firm was in trouble now, just as Joe's had been three years ago. Alex had watched all this develop from a distance, seeing the signs of trouble and knowing the answer, but knowing too that it never paid to try to force help where it wasn't requested.

It was requested now. So as Joe and Becky danced, and the partners paused to give them a spontaneous round of applause, Alex counseled his old roommate and friend. "I don't know if I'm the right guy to help you," he said candidly. "We've known each other so long, and our past might get in the way. It might make more sense to hook you up with someone else who's been through it before, who can teach you as I've taught him. I have someone specific in mind. How does that sound to you?"

It sounded fine.

And so the story would come full circle, the one who'd been led taking his own turn to lead.

"Who'd've believed it?" Joe cracked the following morning, once he'd gotten over his shock at Alex's bombshell suggestion. "Me teaching the Practice Growth Model!"

"Yes, but remember," Alex chided him gently. "The key to success, everything they need to know, is contained within the Model itself. All you have to do is help them discover it."

THE PRACTICE GROWTH MODEL

For as long as anyone can remember, the process through which accountants *deliver* work has been more sophisticated than the *practice-growth* side. In fact, in many firms, practice growth is perceived as an extracurricular activity, to be undertaken only after all the billable hours have been executed. That inequity must be righted in order to allow firms to grow efficiently and effectively. As leader of your CPA firm—be it a solo practice or a practice with many partners—you need to ask yourself this question: Do I want practice growth to remain tangential to core business, or is it time to bring it out of the extracurricular realm and make it part of the core curriculum?

The model Alex refers to in this book—the Practice Growth Model— provides the framework for building a high-growth culture in your firm. Every business discipline is based on foundational concepts, and growth is no different. Just as we all learned in Accounting 101 that debits and credits always equal each other, and that debits are always left and credits right, there are similar foundational constructs associated with growth. Once understood, they make implementation more effective and efficient. Things work the way they're supposed to. And growth isn't an ever-elusive mystery.

In consulting with CPA firms, I've discovered that very few have knowledge of the underpinnings that a consistent growth initiative requires. I also know, from my work with these firms over the years, that operating within a framework builds direction and purpose. Thus, the Practice Growth Model helps firms identify where they are, and where they are headed, at any given time. It enables firm leaders to speak to each other in a common growth language, to understand the implications of actions, and to share a clear point of reference for implementation.

The Model has evolved, becoming simpler and easier to use over time. (It was Picasso who said it took him a lifetime to paint like a child!) We've all seen too many systems that scream complexity. Festooned with boxes and arrows in all directions, they're enough to make one dizzy, and they're intimidating to use. The best models allow efficient execution. So I've stripped the Practice Growth Model down to four elements, or levers, which build upon the four stages of the rainmaking process.

Don't be fooled by the simplicity of the Model. Sustained and efficient growth will come only when the right initiatives are properly implemented within it. Approaching business growth systematically can reap big rewards. You'll spend less time and get better results, avoiding tactical time-wasting activities that aren't part of the plan.

The foundation of the Model is the rainmaking process. Each stage in this process requires its own skill set, its own processes, and its own metrics. Firms that don't understand this run the risk of wasting time and money hiring the wrong people to carry out each task—like hiring a tax person and asking him to execute an audit. In the same vein, when firms commit to "sales training," they may not realize that training in segmenting, targeting, and positioning is quite different from training in lead generation. And both are distinctly different from training for opportunity development.

The result of this muddled approach is a firm that has holes and disconnected tactics throughout its practice growth efforts. The ultimate result is wasted resources and suboptimal return on investments. Typical manifestations include:

- Campaigns that come and go—firms that don't build on experience to develop a meaningful understanding of growth
- No consistent frame of reference to illuminate where the firm is in the building process

- Spotty implementation, in which certain things are implemented and others are not
- No common language to enable discussion of growth initiatives within the partner group
- No handing down of knowledge from one generation to the next

When a firm segues from an approach where individuals just "get out there and do good work" to one where all the parts are coordinated, growth is optimized. In the corporate world, the vice presidents of sales, marketing, and product management become the glue, the ones who ensure that all field people are coordinating their efforts to drive revenue. Can you imagine a bunch of salespeople in a company that had no leader driving processes, metrics, behaviors, coaching, mentoring, and providing help with large opportunities? Yet in many CPA firms, this is what the "growth initiative" looks like.

When efforts are coordinated, however, results appear. Your firm's marketing people will focus mainly on revenue growth activities. Partners will spend fewer hours developing business, but receive a higher dollar-value return. You'll find that *everyone* involved in growth—marketing, sales, and partners—will interface better, understanding where their responsibilities fit, and providing seamless handoffs to others. Finally, your firm will be more competitive, better positioned in the market, ready to take advantage of more opportunities for developing new services and industries in the future.

So let's take a closer look at the rainmaking process and the Practice Growth Model. The foundation of the Model is the rainmaking process, shown next.

Step 1. *Segmenting/targeting/positioning (STP)*. The goal here is to segment, target, and position your firm favorably with regard to your target markets. This work supports each of the other stages. Done correctly, it leads to the second step.

Step 2. *Lead generation*. This stage focuses on developing and nurturing quality contacts within a specific "ecosystem." Some of these contacts will have needs that match your offerings at

The Rainmaking Process

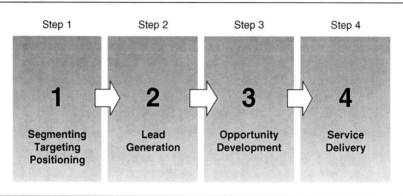

some point in time. Executed properly, lead generation will lead to the third step.

Step 3. *Opportunity development.* The aim here is to continually develop and effectively manage the right opportunities—those that have the most potential and are strategically important—with the right resources. When opportunities are managed properly, the firm will achieve the highest win rate possible, leading to the fourth stage.

Step 4. *Service delivery.* This is where it all comes together—perfecting and delivering focused service offerings that meet the clients' needs. This is the stage of the rainmaking process in which most professionals excel. CPAs have spent decades fine-tuning service delivery methodologies, resource deployment, quality control, and efficiency measures. The key for most firms is to develop the first three stages of the process, to bring the sophistication in those areas to the level we've already achieved in service delivery. This is what the Practice Growth Model is all about.

Space prohibits a full discussion of the rainmaking process. However, the execution of the four steps is only the *foundation* of firm activity. The way to optimize growth is to *manage* the process. And this is where the Practice Growth Model comes in. The Model consists of four distinct levers, or methods of growth management. Carried out effectively, the synergistic effect of these levers can be significant. A firm's managing partner and other leaders can use the levers to boost the firm's overall performance. Just as professional service firms have managed Step 4—service delivery—for decades, CPAs can now manage the entire Model, to enable the growth side to attain the same level of sophistication as the delivery side.

The four levers of the Practice Growth Model are marketing, industry niche management, service line management, and large opportunity management. As shown in the next diagram, the levers address management of various steps in the rainmaking process.

The Practice Growth Model

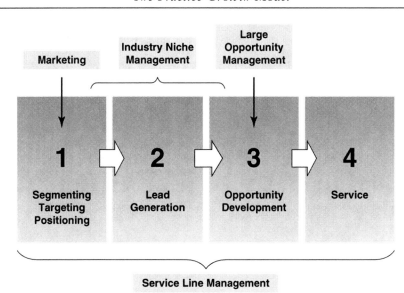

Marketing

Hewlett-Packard founder David Packard once said, "Marketing is too important to be left up to the marketing department." Yet many professional services firms park marketing responsibility at the doorstep of the firm's marketing director and concern themselves mainly with delivering good work. But in order for the Growth Model to work, two things need to happen. First, partners need to work properly with marketing (more about this later). Second, the marketing director must grow past marketing, into affecting practice growth.

The great myth is that marketing drives revenue. I was recently invited to speak about driving marketing efforts into top-line revenue. I explained that I couldn't do it, because this simply isn't how it works. Marketing is not a discipline designed to yield revenue. Marketing is all about long-term strategy, and involves segmenting, targeting, and positioning. If the marketing investment is buttressed with proper conversion elbow grease (lead generation and opportunity development activities), revenue will follow. Proper conversion means that someone needs to leverage the marketing investment into leads and then sell something. Simply put, the goal of marketing is to segment, target, and position your firm in relation to your target markets. Marketing represents the tilling of the soil to support each of the other stages. Done correctly, marketing leads to the second step of the Practice Growth Model.

A few years ago, *Inside Public Accounting*'s Benchmarking Report noted that the average fee growth for firms in the survey was approximately the same, *whether the firm had marketing professionals on board or not*. I rest my case.

One observation I've made in working with countless marketing directors is that many of them are stuck with tactical marketing communications activities—affectionately known in corporate America as "marcomm." The personal growth and effect they can have on firms is limited, often due to lack of understanding about the next level of effectiveness they might achieve. Instead of perpetuating this limited approach, firms need to allow the position to evolve into a *strategic* resource that will provide high-value guidance and direction.

By attracting—or developing—the right person with the right experience, the firm can bring to the table not just someone who can create brochures, but someone who can create business opportunities. So the goal is to foster an environment in which a marketing director can contribute as much as partners in the planning and implementation of a growth plan.

Again, it's not just about the qualifications of the person in the job, but about giving that person the opportunity to contribute fully. This integration may require some reeducation of your partners, but it's well worth the effort.

Which came first—the chicken or the egg? Are marketing directors stuck in tactical execution because they aren't asked to the table during the firm's strategic growth discussions, or are they left out of these discussions because they aren't perceived as experienced enough to contribute? It makes no difference. The end result is that many directors of marketing are shackled and relegated to suboptimization—of their own efforts, as well as their potential effect on the firm. And an unfortunate result is the realization on their part that their discipline is perceived as fluffy, immaterial, of secondary importance, a necessary evil. They then have an uncomfortable feeling that they're perceived as second-class citizens.

Many directors have their hands tied—by administrative work, lack of support staff, insufficient budget, and a general inability to get their hands on financial information they need, but is deemed confidential and thus inaccessible—to the very director who is charged with supporting revenue growth! More often than not, I hear, under their breath and with the door closed, that the CPAs "just don't get it." I remember when a network engineer accused me of not "getting it" several years ago, when I was in the telecommunications business. Ouch! That hurt!

So let me create a vision of what a very senior practice growth expert looks like. This person creates and understands the strategy behind what drives firm growth. He or she understands intimately the appropriate roles of marketing, industry niche management, opportunity management, and service line management—the disciplines that make up practice growth. He or she can advise the firm on resource deployment alternatives that will yield optimal revenue growth.

This person is compensated based on overall firm growth, not tactical efforts. The person might have come up through any of a number of subdisciplines associated with practice growth, but has been able to stretch horizontally and add understanding and experience in related disciplines. As a result, he or she has touched (performed, managed, or been responsible for) virtually all of these areas: marketing strategy, marketing communications (including public relations and advertising), lead generation, opportunity development (including lead qualification and developing and closing opportunities), and product management.

If your marketing director doesn't sound like this person, there is plenty of room for career development, and there are many opportunities for your director to develop these competencies within the typical medium and large CPA firm—especially in today's turbulent environment, which requires a sharp competitive ax.

My suggestion is that you first change the title from director of marketing to director of practice growth, to reflect the enhanced role and expectations that apply to the next generation of marketing executives. Next, include him or her in all partner meetings of strategic content, even if only as an observer. Marketing directors who have the potential will rise to the strategic level—but only if they are specifically included in strategic matters. Linking practice growth strategy to invested practice growth resource is critical to getting the bang for your marketing director buck. Ask your newly renamed director of practice growth to rewrite the job description, including goals and compensation scheme. Tie the person's goals and compensation directly to practice growth. This will get rid of the nice-to-have marketing initiatives that don't contribute to increasing revenue.

Industry Niche Management and Service Line Management

Two other important levers in the Growth Model are the management of industry niches and service lines. The roles are similar, yet there are a few differences. The Model shows that industry niche management is, first and foremost, concerned with lead generation. But it also involves the marketing function in segmenting/targeting/positioning and working with partners to develop opportunities within the industry niche. Industry niches are the best way to generate leads, because industries (and other segmented buyer groups) best define distinct ecosystems. People in them tend to hang out together, buyers have similar needs, and solutions can be better tailored to specific buyer groups. This enables a highly efficient client acquisition approach.

Service line management is concerned with all phases of the Model. Unfortunately, most heads of service lines are concerned only with Step 4, service delivery. But someone in the firm needs to be concerned with all phases of the Model, in the form of ensuring that the right services are being brought to market, and brought to market in the right way. Service line leaders need to work closely with industry niche leaders, to make sure the right services are in place to solve buyer problems, thereby optimizing lead generation.

I describe both industry niche leaders and service line leaders generically as segment leaders, because each of their areas of focus represents a segment of the firm's revenues. And the starting point for management of segments is to segment the firm's revenues by industry and service line and assign leaders to each.

Segmenting revenues starts a firm down the road of segment leadership. The next task is to build a spreadsheet on which services are rows and industries are columns. Run the total down the right-hand side and across the bottom, and list the individuals assigned to each segment. If your system can produce the numbers, fill in the spreadsheet to show the intersection of revenue segments by industry and service line, as shown in the next example.

This exercise almost always reveals surprises. The relationship of revenue segments to each other is important. It helps firm leaders make decisions and trade off alternatives in a way that's more informed and enhances the overall good of the firm.

Service Lines	Industry 1	Industry 2	Industry 3	All Other	Total	Owner
Audit	$3,500	$2,000	$1,000	$7,500	$14,000	John
Compile & Write-up	$125	$250	$450	$278	$1,103	Sally
Corporate Tax	$2,000	$1,575	$1,675	$1,450	$6,700	Sue
Individual Tax	$1,380	$1,520	$250	$1,675	$4,825	Paul
Other 1	$150	$245	$650	$850	$1,895	Joe
Other 2	$25	$65	$450	$225	$765	Mary
Other 3	$450	$125	$165	$163	$903	Kelly
Total	$7,630	$5,780	$4,640	$12,141	$30,191	
Owner	Sharon	Richard	Sam	Jeff		

The segmentation of revenue and establishment of growth goals arranged by segment are tools to help the managing partner effectively manage the firm's revenue growth.

Of course, segmented revenue growth metrics seldom appear in the framework of a typical CPA firm, so some effort may be required to establish and confirm the segments, identify and assign segment growth goals, and develop a compensation scheme for segment leaders that makes sense.

However, there are many advantages to this approach.

- It undermines the unhelpful book-of-business mentality that reigns in most firms. In this model, partners acquire and manage their own clients, and clients are seldom seen as assets of the firm. Any attempt to land a new opportunity is an individual—and often lonely— experience. So in this model, firms suffer, because very little synergy and organization-wide knowledge of business development is developed within the firm.
- This approach lends greater structure to lead generation efforts.
- It provides opportunities for segment owners to develop leadership skills. It creates the structure and methodology necessary to approach the market in a more coordinated way.

- It promotes innovation in the firm's services and keeps the services relevant to market conditions.
- It enables the firm to identify market trends more quickly and make better, more efficient decisions about new services or industry niches.
- It enables the firm to pursue larger clients and lessens the emphasis on less profitable ones.
- It makes it possible for partners and managers to contribute to firm growth in ways that are more effective than in traditional marketing communications or lead generation campaigns, which are sometimes only marginally effective.

To strengthen ownership and results, it is necessary to develop segment leader knowledge of product management, which is the functional discipline being drawn on when services are brought to market successfully, and to keep that knowledge relevant to markets. Most firms believe marketing and sales functions are required for growth, even though some firms misunderstand marketing and sales, thinking they're the same. But with the exception of the very largest CPA firms, product management remains a function about which there is very little knowledge. The result is that a firm will be wildly successful in one or a few segments, while others die on the vine.

Yet the same discipline—product management—can be applied to *all* segments to achieve consistent success. The years I spent at IBM taught me this. We had product managers for each of our computer products, peripheral devices, software packages, and so forth. We used disciplined product management techniques to ensure consistent success across all our product lines.

Similar techniques can be applied to professional services. And it's more than just the promotion of an offering. It's the process of identifying prospect needs, determining the perfect prospect profile, identifying and describing overall concept and methodology, identifying major components of the service, determining the value proposition for marketplace "positioning," and identifying the best way to commercialize it.

Many of these activities must be performed by a partner. Marketing people can help, but the partner knows the buyer and service best. Note, too, that many of these activities don't fall within the traditional definition of sales or marketing. Because market conditions are always changing—due to regulation, competition, or technology—service line management is a dynamic activity. What happens when no one manages a firm's service lines? It misses new market opportunities—SOX 404, SAS 70, forensic, international. In fact, many firms *have* missed these lucrative opportunities because there was no service line management responsibility in place.

The overall responsibility of the service line or industry niche leader is to provide strategic direction and optimize the financial health of the segment. This includes identifying new services and markets. It also includes leading, coordinating, and/or managing resources and processes to achieve stated service line or niche objectives. Financial health includes year-over-year revenue and margin growth of a service, bundle of services, or industry niche. Service line and industry niche leaders should be rewarded financially for bearing responsibility for growth in these segments. Strict definitions of ownership, compensation, and role clarity will provide the structure necessary for leaders to drive their segments.

Interestingly, the competencies needed for solid service line management are analytical, strategic, and leadership skills—just as with product management in corporate America. Before IBM allowed individuals coming out of the field to secure their first management jobs, they had to serve time as an industry or product manager and display those competencies. They had to show that they could work through others to accomplish the financial objectives of their product or industry, even if those "others" didn't report to them directly. All industry and product managers came out of the field, and were technical and salespeople who understood the client. This responsibility was never put in the hands of marketing people who hadn't been intimately involved with delivering products and services to clients.

Developing a strategic direction involves deciding which services to offer, which distribution channels are best, and the likely profile of targeted prospects (as shown in the next diagram). Every ecosystem is unique in this regard. Different ecosystems value different services, use different distribution channels, and contain different types of targeted prospects. That's why attacking the broader market by identifying different ecosystems and working with each of them differently is so powerful.

Firms that still look at their market as one big marketplace are out of sync with where the CPA profession is today. When the profession was younger, CPAs could merely hang out a shingle. But with maturity came buyer and competitor sophistication. The conversation today is not about whether to pursue market niches or not. The question is simply which niches to pursue.

Developing a Strategic Direction

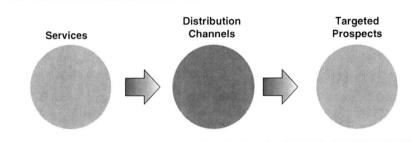

Services | Distribution Channels | Targeted Prospects

Segment leaders also have the responsibility of establishing and monitoring revenue and profitability goals. Incentive compensation for the segment leader should be based on attainment of discrete goals, plus qualitative assessment of goals. But if the firm is new to segment management, it will take time for segment leaders to learn product management techniques and apply them to their segments, so proper time should be allowed before they are held accountable for revenue results.

One important leadership task of the segment leaders is to assemble the appropriate team, assign responsibilities, monitor progress, and modify strategy and tactics to achieve revenue objectives. Segment leader responsibility is sometimes the first opportunity certain partners have to affect a firm-wide initiative. Many have been involved with clients and their own book of business. But the firm needs leaders who can take a segment of the revenue and manage it. As a result, segment leadership naturally enables partners to develop their leadership skills in a very important way.

Opportunity Management

Opportunity management is the lever that enables the managing partner and partner group to manage the entire inventory of important opportunities. However, it's not helpful to overmanage every last opportunity within the firm. The organic, smaller, noncompetitive opportunities that occur naturally hardly require more than a partner's continuing oversight. But when opportunities are larger, competitive, or strategically significant, the firm as a whole has more to win or lose by their proper management. Moreover, the firm will always have a given number of active opportunities and limited resources to apply to them. So it's imperative that these opportunities be managed effectively.

There are firms that have changed their cultures to become expert at harvesting significant opportunities and consistently boosting win rates. They've done it by implementing a few key steps:

- Develop an effective pipeline and pipeline process.
- Train partners in winning larger opportunities.
- Hold quarterly internal client opportunity reviews for the largest clients.

Additionally, larger firms have effectively integrated one or more professional business developers (salespeople).

Stages 1 and 2 of the rainmaking cycle are designed to create demand; they place emphasis on niche development. When the pump is primed, though, it's time to shift to sophisticated opportunity management.

Large opportunities should be perceived as assets of the firm, not as part of an individual partner's book of business. When opportunity management is not evident in a firm, the evidence is there in abundance.

- Partners pursue larger opportunities with the same methods as smaller ones, despite the fact that the proper technique for each is different.

- Opportunities fall through the cracks.
- There is no succinct, easy-to-understand pipeline showing what's being pursued.
- The firm has proposal logs (inventories of late-stage opportunities where there is little ability to influence outcomes) rather than pipelines (which include early-stage opportunities that enable substantial influence on outcomes).
- Smaller, low-odds opportunities take the same priority as larger, more strategic opportunities.
- Opportunities get stuck for weeks or months, with no apparent movement through the opportunity cycle.
- There is lack of clarity about next steps, masquerading also as "We're waiting for the prospect to respond."
- Business developers are suboptimized (then later questioned about whether they're adding value).

Instead, envision a firm that embraces opportunity development, where the large pieces of business are pursued with the same level of sophistication as service delivery is. With knowledge and proper execution, that firm can be your own.

Developing a new culture starts with *properly* implementing a large-opportunity pipeline. *The pipeline is the financial statement of opportunity management*—an inventory of all large, active opportunities the firm is currently pursuing. No executive would run a firm without a balance sheet and income statement. The pipeline represents the same powerful report for opportunity management. It can be produced in Excel or with a CRM software package. The purpose of the pipeline is to give the firm's partner group a precise overview of large opportunities. It lets them know what's happening and who's making it happen.

But make no mistake—the pipeline is anything but a static, passive document. Developed and used properly, it is a dynamic business-building tool.

A pipeline differs significantly from a proposal log, which is simply a reactive record. The proposal log has limited value because by the time a proposal is issued, the selling window is closing. In fact, 80 to 90 percent of persuasive communication occurs *before* the proposal leaves the firm's hands. After that, there is very little opportunity to influence the prospective client.

A disciplined approach to managing opportunities creates a strategy for future growth, and it also works to eliminate waste. When everyone is working together and knows what business is being pursued and by whom, there's significantly less duplication of effort. Moreover, minimal effort is expended on lesser opportunities. Since most firms' resources are already stretched, educating the partner group about the inventory of active opportunities will enable the firm to make more informed decisions about resource allocation.

Deciding which business to pursue is always critical, as these decisions will shape the client base down the road. A well-managed pipeline process is a cornerstone for effective decision making about which opportunities to pursue. The goal is to put in place a tightly structured pipeline that shows the opportunities being pursued, their strategic significance, potential revenue, and likely closing date.

I've seen many pipeline processes, some great and many weak. The difference between creating meaningful cultural change and just adding another report to fill out lies in the quality of the pipeline process, the centerpiece of which is the pipeline review.

The pipeline review is simply that—a meeting in which the pipeline is examined and discussed. The review typically takes place twice monthly in a teleconference among partners and is led by the managing partner. Before and during the review session, the partners work to update the pipeline, aided by an administrative person who compiles and disseminates the results.

Pipeline reviews evolve, from simply sharing what's happening where, to a process involving assigning a value to each pursuit. Positive peer pressure increases pipeline activity by encouraging partners to drive opportunities. Congratulating opportunity leaders and inviting them to share their winning strategies adds to the collective knowledge of the group. This in turn leads to a higher-quality effort, greater resource deployment, and, ultimately, a higher win rate for the firm. Losses are presented as teaching moments, rather than embarrassing personal failures.

The next important step in building the opportunity development process is training. At this point, partners who have honed skills in other areas often recognize the need for specific instruction in the pursuit of high-quality opportunities. Just as in carrying out delivery of a tax or audit project, landing large business requires specific skills and knowledge.

Training includes teaching partners how to function as a coordinated team, improving the quality of the opportunity process, and increasing their understanding of strategies used to close opportunities. Which methods will provide an edge over competitors, or keep them at bay? As partners are trained, they continually learn from each other, adding constantly to the firm's collective knowledge. They become knowledgeable about the firm's competitors and their strategies and winning approaches. Training also provides a common language for pursing major opportunities. Sharing this vocabulary—which includes such phrases as "qualified versus unqualified," "triangulating," and "recalibrating"— helps a team work more efficiently toward common goals. This can lead to more sharply focused initiatives and, ultimately, greater success in pursuing opportunities.

Large opportunity training is different from generic sales training, because large opportunities are more complex and competitive. Multiple decision makers with different objectives create political situations that the pursuit team must understand and navigate. A firm might have the best solution and best pricing among all competitors, but if it's not aware that it represents a choice among the decision makers with certain implications, it won't win the opportunity. Firms competing for opportunities are always battling competitors with preexisting relationships. Buyers might be trading off this consideration with others. One decision maker, for example, might want a different type of firm because of historical experience. In reality, there are countless factors that affect large opportunities, and the skill lies in uncovering them during the pursuit. In addition, most large opportunities have a definitive, and sometimes short, time frame. So all this work needs to get done while racing the clock!

This is a much different scenario from lead generation, where partners and firms can languish for months or years, developing trusting relationships with potential buyers. Large opportunity management makes the process much different from lead generation. Lead generation is akin to noncurrent assets, whereas opportunity development is more like current assets. Just as these assets are managed differently, so must the two sets of activities be managed differently.

The final process in opportunity management is to hold quarterly internal opportunity reviews of the firm's largest clients.

Consider this: In the average midmarket CPA firm, 39 percent of firm revenue is generated by 39 clients, with an average of two to four service offerings per client. Managing this top tier, since it represents a significant source of revenue, must become a high priority. Identify those clients (it may be 19 or 49 percent at your firm) and manage them just as the assets of your balance sheet are managed. Regularly assess your efforts with your top clients by holding internal reviews on one-quarter of your large clients each quarter, and be sure to include every member of the team who can contribute ideas concerning optimizing service and uncovering additional opportunities.

Devote about an hour to discussing and validating a strategic plan for each client. This will keep everyone up to date on current opportunities in the client base and give partners an opportunity to contribute to the growth of these large clients.

We did this religiously when I worked at IBM. Virtually all our new revenue came from current clients, so it became imperative to identify opportunities and work them vigorously. Internal client reviews were the planning mechanism used to make sure everyone on the team was involved and executing the right revenue growth plans. Since certain accounts had more potential in any given year than others, this approach allowed us to keep our focus on those clients and kept us from wasting time with clients where there was little opportunity.

Where lead generation and opportunity development are concerned, many larger and midmarket firms use professional business development people to support the firm's efforts. Business developers have years of full-time experience in selling and thus are able to determine quickly and efficiently which leads represent the highest-quality opportunities and which will be easiest to close. Despite their technical and occasional rainmaking prowess, partners, overworked as they are, may make three or four calls on a prospect, or perhaps even complete the sales cycle, before concluding that there's nothing there.

But business development people are *specialists*, with skills that go far beyond basic relationship development. Effective business developers are also persuasive communicators who are capable of delving deep below the surface to identify not only professional objectives, but personal agendas as well. Thus, they can build unique value propositions that link personal and professional objectives, and in so doing develop a winning strategy. In situations where your technical resources may not be as deep as your competitor's, a savvy business developer will be able to muster the skills to close business from the underdog position. It's part of their DNA and their training!

Every business development transaction involves two things—establishing technical credentials and developing a relationship. Some partners may be expert in one, but not both. Using a business developer frees them to do what they do best. Top rainmaker partners, aging with the rest of us, are often not plentiful enough to sustain future growth in many firms. Business developers offer a solid alternative. They make it possible to provide realistic retirement, and to attract and retain highly qualified staff.

To be successful, though, they must be allowed to become part of the firm's infrastructure and leadership. Partners must check their egos at the door and come to grips with the fact that someone who develops business full time is a specialist.

Finally, let's look at the bottom-line rationale. If a partner who bills out at $300 an hour spends two hours each week on business development, that's a $30,000 investment. Multiply that by the number of partners in your firm, and that's how much you may be spending on business development, relying on partners who may be only marginally effective in this area.

If you reallocate a percentage of that to hire a business developer, you've wisely reinvested those resources. A good business developer will likely pay for him- or herself within 12 to 18months. It may take a partner 20 or 30 years to build up an annual revenue stream of $2 million, but a good business developer can secure annualized revenue of $500,000 to $1 million and more.

These, then, are the four levers of practice growth: marketing, industry niche management, service line management, and large opportunity management. Effectively managing each of them will optimize your efforts. In addition, you'll be covering all the elements of the Practice Growth Model, to achieve a synergistic effect among the components.

Too many firms get religion about pursuing marketing but don't balance those efforts with initiatives in niche management, service offering management, and opportunity management. Yet all these components are critical to managing revenue generation for CPA firms. To use a stage analogy, they are critical to your production. A firm that spends marketing dollars positioning itself and creating awareness, but doesn't invest equally in developing and landing opportunities and keeping its offerings fresh and market relevant, is likely to fail in its pursuit of optimal revenue growth. As you structure your revenue growth initiatives, commit to making investments in *all* these important areas.

As you tackle revenue growth, your best foot forward is a collective one. Yes, you do give up some individual independence. But consider the benefits—an exciting growth environment that attracts top candidates and secures the firm's financial future. Ultimately, there's very little room for prima donnas in the work of pursuing growth, just dedicated team members who shine brightest when they shine together.

CPSIA information can be obtained at www.ICGtesting.com
Printed in the USA
BVOW012107120412

287488BV00008B/121/P